FEARLESS

The Complete Personal Safety Guide for Women

Fearless: The Complete Personal Safety Guide for Women offers extensive practical advice on personal safety and a variety of effective self-defence strategies. While presenting the reader with material on safety awareness and effective physical and non-physical resistance techniques, Paul Henry Danylewich also investigates the social patterns of sexual assault and domestic violence, drawing on interviews with fifty sex offenders as well as resources provided by law enforcement agencies, rape crisis centres, hospitals, and public safety organizations in North America.

Danylewich, the director of an organization specializing in safety issues for women, argues that women in general are not conditioned or socialized adequately to defend themselves in threatening situations. He offers prevention tips to reduce an individual's chances of becoming the target of an aggressor and debunks myths surrounding sexual assault. He describes in detail techniques for reducing the likelihood of being victimized in various circumstances, including dating, driving alone, working late, walking alone, taking public transit, and answering the phone or the front door at home. To help women learn these easy and effective self-defence techniques, the guide is illustrated with over 140 action photos.

Fearless contains information every woman should have to help her live more safely and with less fear. This guide is a complete personal safety manual that can empower women, providing them with the resources necessary to help recognize and avoid potentially violent situations.

PAUL HENRY DANYLEWICH has been teaching self-defence techniques over the years to thousands of women in North America in his capacity as Director and Counselor, White Tiger Street Defense.

FEARLESS

The Complete Personal Safety Guide for Women

Paul Henry Danylewich

UNIVERSITY OF TORONTO PRESS

Toronto Buffalo London

© University of Toronto Press Incorporated 2001
Toronto Buffalo London
ISBN 0-7394-2589-7

The University of Toronto Press acknowledges the financial assistance to its publishing program of the Canada Council for the Arts and the Ontario Arts Council.

University of Toronto Press acknowledges the financial support for its publishing activities of the Government of Canada through the Book Publishing Industry Development Program (BPIDP).

This book is dedicated to my son, Justin Dean.

Contents

Preface

The content of this guide is based on different types of sources in order to provide the reader with a comprehensive understanding of how potentially violent situations can be recognized and possibly avoided. The book is based on an academic framework. Insights gathered from interviews with rape survivors and prevention information supplied by law enforcement officials are also reflected in this book. In addition, information gathered from inmate interviews is included in order to present the offender's perspective on how to reduce the risk of being targeted and attacked. Fifty convicted sex offenders from Clinton Correctional Facility (Dannemora, NY), Bear Hill Correctional Facility (Malone, NY), Franklin Correctional Facility (Malone, NY), and Northwest State Correctional Facility (Saint Albans, VT) were interviewed.

I would like to thank all of the police officers, survivors, prison inmates, parents, teachers, and students who have provided their personal stories and views about assault prevention.

Acknowledgments

I would like to express a special thank you to my wife, Eliana, who has helped me through the development of this book, and who has truly inspired me to make my dream a reality.

I would also like to thank all the members of White Tiger Street Defense for sticking with me through good times and bad: Claudia Saheb, Glenn Bolan, Antonietta Mannarino, Nancy Boulé, and Nancy Leger.

All of the team members have made great sacrifices in their personal and professional lives to learn and understand issues surrounding violence against women and children. I respect their commitment, and I am grateful for each of their contributions.

The following individuals deserve special recognition for helping me develop this book: Professor Neil Malamuth and Professor J. Goodchilds, University of California at Los Angeles; Professor Sarah E. Ullman, University of Illinois at Chicago; Donald G. Lyon, Deputy Chief (Ret.), Ottawa-Carleton Regional Police Service, Ottawa; Cynthia J. Lent, National Center for the Analysis of Violent Crime, FBI Academy, Quantico, Virginia; G. Cummings, Center for the Treatment of Sex Abusers, Vermont State Department of Corrections, St Albans, Vermont; Linda Folio, Public Information Office, New York State Department of Corrections, Albany; M.-J. Adelman, New York State Police, Albany; Tpr. D. Cogan, New York State Police, Chazy, New York; Det. T. Anderson, Rutland Police Department, Rutland, Vermont; Lt. Mark W. Sparks, University of Maryland Police, College Park, Maryland; Betty Petropolous, Shield of Athena, Montreal; Maj. Linda Flood, Baltimore School Police Force, Baltimore; Staff Insp. E.C. Ludlow, Metropolitan Toronto Police; Staff Sgt. J.M. Templeton, Edmonton Police Service, Edmonton, Alberta; PO Helen Citrano, University of California at Los Angeles Campus Police; Diane Blanchette, Dean of Student Affairs Office, Bishops University, Lennoxville, Quebec; Captain M.J. Johnson, Metropolitan Police Department, Washington, DC; Sgt. E.C. Snow, Royal Newfoundland Constabulary, St John's; Chief J.F. Croughwell, Hartford Police Department, Hartford; Connecticut; Jen Engel, Orange County Rape Crisis Center, Chapel Hill,

North Carolina; Com. E.N. Christia, Chicago Police Department; Chief J. Adkin, Windsor Police Service, Windsor, Ontario; J. Lake, Victim Services Program, Newfoundland Department of Justice, St John's; Det. F.J. Romaine, Rape Special Section, Los Angeles Police Department; Kim Phinny, Women's Rape Crisis Center, Burlington, Vermont; Emmett M. Will, Canadian Police College, Ottawa; Maj. K.H. Taylor, Tampa Police Department, Tampa, Florida; M. Rosales, Connecticut State Department of Public Safety; Deborah Tenino, Rape Treatment Center of Santa Monica Hospital Medical Center, Santa Monica, California; Marion Boyd, Minister Responsible for Women's Issues and Attorney General, Province of Ontario, Toronto; Sgt. R. Lefebvre, Sudbury Regional Police, Sudbury, Ontario; Sgt. Ken Leendertse, Hamilton-Wentworth Regional Police, Hamilton, Ontario; Anthony D. Bourbon, Associate Director, Violence Prevention Coalition of Greater Los Angeles; J.M. Hughes, Salt Lake City Police Department, Salt Lake City, Utah; and PO Roger Austin, Tempe Police Department, Tempe, Arizona.

FEARLESS

The Complete Personal Safety Guide for Women

Introduction

Violence against women occurs in overwhelming proportions throughout the world. It is not just a women's issue, it is a community issue that affects us all – men, women, and children. Violence or even the threat of violence has the potential to produce a level of fear that can control people's lives. The number of women who live in fear of becoming the next crime statistic increases on a daily basis. Most of us know at least one person (a friend, family member, or acquaintance) who has been the victim of a violent crime. We are all somehow touched by violence. These experiences instil fear in us. Fear creates feelings of powerlessness. It feeds on our innermost vulnerabilities. The threat of losing control over our body, our dignity, and our identity is a terrifying thought. We all have the right to stay safe. This is a basic human right.

Male aggression is fundamentally problematic. It cannot be tolerated or ignored. While aggressors are solely responsible for the violence they perpetrate, society needs to take action to bring this issue to justice. Schools must combat this problem in the classroom. From an early age, males need to understand that violence and abuse are not socially acceptable. They must be encouraged to use non-violent methods of interaction and problem solving.

Victims are in no way responsible for the violence they experience. Learning to recognize violence and the context in which it may occur is an essential tool in reducing its prevalence. Learning ways to reduce the risk of violence can have an empowering impact on us all. The grim reality is that assault prevention education is an essential life skill required to survive in today's world.

Knowledge is power. The objective of this guide is to help you gain the knowledge that is needed to avoid violence. Learning to 'fight' may serve as a strong deterrent in an assault, but mental preparation is also important. Throughout this book, you will be encouraged to adopt a frame of mind that will allow you to reduce the threat of violence. You will realize that it is possible to protect yourself and to live without constant fear.

TIPS FOR BEST USING THIS MANUAL

The intent of this guide is to provide you with a basic knowledge and understanding of self-defence. It is intended to be a supplemental aid, rather than a substitute for an actual self-defence course. As you practise the techniques in this book, decide what you can realistically do. Explore your strengths and weaknesses. Think about how different assaults can happen to you, and develop a plan of how you would respond in each situation. Self-defence guides can be a very useful tool in learning self-defence. However, if you wish to gain greater knowledge of the subject, enrolling in a self-defence class or seminar will be necessary.

Section 1: General Awareness Strategies

Enhancing security in your home is the first step in preventing crime. If it is not done properly, many devices designed to keep burglars out can serve as death traps instead, confining you and your family inside your residence. It is recommended that you consult with your local fire department concerning any changes or upgrades that you are considering or have already made to your home.

Windows

House burglars often break in through a basement window, usually one in the rear of the house that cannot easily be seen from the street. As a deterrence, consider installing metal burglar bars in these windows. They should be installed between the glass panes or on the inside of the window, rather than on the exterior of the house. An exterior installation may require less time on your part, but will not be difficult for burglars to remove. Using the wrong materials for this installation can create a fire escape hazard for your family. Some newer models have an emergency release feature allowing an avenue of escape in case of fire.

Sliding or double-hung windows should be secured. They can either be pinned or simply secured by placing a wooden rod tightly in the window's track. Pinning is probably a better option but requires more time. First, you would need to drill a hole through the top of the window frame. Then insert a metal pin or nail. Louvre-type windows should be replaced by solid panes of glass or another type of window. Crank or casement windows can be secured in a similar way by using an L-type bracket screwed to the lower part of the window. Drill a hole through the bracket into the sill. Then, insert a metal pin or nail into the sill. Make sure to draw curtains and blinds during the evening hours. As a safeguard, you may choose to inspect how much a potential aggressor can see looking in from the outside into your windows with the blinds or curtains drawn. If the curtains are old and thin, consider replacing them with a heavier fabric Be sure to keep all windows free from bushes and tree branches.

Front Doors

Front doors of any residence should open inward, so that the door hinges are not visible from the outside when the door is closed. These doors should be about one and a half inches thick and solid rather than with a hollow core. In apartment buildings or residence halls, always lock doors to common areas such as access doors from garage entrances to lobbies and fire doors. If you see an individual who appears to be waiting, or approaches as you near the access door, do not let the person into the building. Pretend that you have forgotten your keys and leave. Another possible option is to ring your own apartment; when no one answers, leave and report the suspicious person to the police from a safe location. Never let a stranger gain access to the building even if he asks to leave a package for a neighbour. Keep doors locked even when you are in your home.

Locks

The standard centre pin of the knob lock on an exterior door will not provide adequate security. It is recommended that you install a deadbolt lock. This lock should be at least one inch thick and one inch long. There are two basic types: those that require a key to lock from inside, and those that lock with a standard rotary knob. If your doors have windows in them or windows bordering the door within two feet of the lock, you are advised to install the keyed option. A word of caution concerning these locks: If the deadbolt is in the locked position and the key is misplaced, you will not be able to open the door, which creates a fire escape hazard for you and your family. For this reason, many people leave the key in the lock when they are home.

If your door is completely solid and there is no window bordering the door frame you may choose to install a standard deadbolt with an interior rotary locking knob. However, you may still want to consider the keyed option, as it would prevent burglars from leaving through the front door once they have entered the home. Many house burglars do not feel comfortable if they have only one avenue of escape out of the house and may cut their visit short.

In most cases the lock withstands pressure, but the door frame itself will give out. Typical strike plates that come with good quality locks should be upgraded if they are not longer than two and a half inches. Screws that are at least two inches long should be used to secure the plate to the door frame. Metal door frames are generally stronger than wood frames. In older homes make sure that the door jamb is solid and that the strike plate is not secured to a rotten wooden frame. For added security you can add an additional deadbolt lock on the backside of the door that can be locked only when you are inside the residence (with no key hole on the exterior side), making it impossible to pick.

Building a Safe Room

Some may consider building a safe room in their house. The general notion behind this concept is that if you are attacked in your own home, you may have an opportunity to run into the safe room, and lock out the assailant while you call for help. It is recommended that you install a deadbolt surface mount lock on the back side of your bedroom or bathroom door, providing there is a window that can act as an escape route out of the room. Bedrooms and bathrooms are the most common choices for safe rooms. For maximum security, treat the safe room door as an exterior door. Since most interior doors are of the hollow core type, it will need to be replaced by a solid wood or metal type. Hinges to this door should not be exposed when the door is closed shut. The door frame and strike plate should be upgraded as well.

Ideally, it would be helpful to install a separate phone line. This line should have a separate entry point away from the entry point installations of existing phone lines in the home. This phone should be hidden in an out of the way place and used only for emergencies. A simple phone extension to the same room will serve as a less safe, low-cost alternative. Storing your cellular phone and charger in the safe room would also help you communicate to authorities in a crisis situation.

Keys

Here are some useful safety guidelines:

- Do not mark your key chain with your name, address, or phone number.
- Be able to easily separate your car keys from your other keys. You may choose to use a detachable key ring for this purpose, or a separate car key ring altogether.
- Do not store spare keys in obvious hiding places such as under entrance welcome mats, in flower pots, or in mailboxes.
- Leave spare keys with someone that you trust in case you are ever locked out.
- It is strongly recommended that you change your locks if your keys are ever stolen or missing. It is also wise to change your locks upon moving into a new residence.
- Try to carry your keys separately from your wallet so that if your wallet is stolen, the perpetrator will not be able to gain entry into your residence.
- Keep in mind that if you purchase a pre-owned automobile the former owner may have made several key copies. Consider changing car door, trunk, and ignition locks for peace of mind.
- Treat a remote control garage door opener as a key. Do not leave it in your vehicle; if stolen it may provide easy access to your home. Likewise, upon moving into a pre-owned home that has a garage door opener already installed, be aware that someone may have a duplicate remote control. This is often overlooked by new home owners.

Lights

Lighting can definitely serve as an inexpensive deterrent to intruders. Consider purchasing motion sensitive exterior lights. These lights automatically turn on when the sensors are triggered by any movement. Install them near all entrances and other vulnerable areas surrounding your residence. Although these lights have a sensitivity setting that can be adjusted, they are likely to be set off by non-human elements even when set on low sensitivity. Wind and rain can create common false alarms. Although they may be falsely set off, motion sensor lights prove to be very useful in a real situation. Dusk to dawn sensor lights also serve as a deterrent against intruders. These lights automatically turn on once the sun sets, and turn off during the early morning. In addition, timers can help deter crime in your home. They can be used to control lights or radios when you are not in. Always try to leave an interior light on when you plan to return home after dark.

Make sure that lights are working properly in apartment complexes or residence halls. Every entrance to your residence should be equipped with an exterior light which should be used every night. Try to position the light about ten feet from the ground with a good quality impact resistant lens cover. This added effort will make it more difficult for an aggressor to break or tamper with the light. If you are home alone, consider turning on lights in more than one room. This will help create the illusion that more than one person is in the residence.

Home Appearance

Keep your landscaping trim and neat, especially around windows and entrances. Neighbours should be able to see vulnerable ground floor windows and entrances from a distance. Your home should have a lived-in look even when you are away. Have neighbours cut your grass and take in your mail. Perhaps even ask a neighbour to park a car in your driveway.

Neighbours

- Get to know your neighbours. They can be your greatest asset to establishing a safe environment for your family. People are much more likely to get involved during a crisis, when the victim is a friend or someone they know.
- Neighbours can provide a safe place to go in case of an emergency.
- Discuss with them what their response should be to yelling and screaming. Perhaps discuss a code system that could be used to signal help from each other. For example, if you live alone and arrive home every evening at 6:30, arrangements could be made with your neighbor that they watch from their window as you open your garage door with your remote control. The neighbors would watch until you have driven into your garage and the door closes.

Alarms

- Consider getting a dog. Even a friendly medium-sized dog that barks at strangers or when the doorbell rings would be a deterrent.
- There are many different types of alarms on the market. Some are hooked up to an outside alarm that requires the goodwill of neighbours to call the police. These systems vary widely in quality standards. Experience and care are needed in the planning, installation, and operation of the unit. Frequent false alarms will desensitize the neighbours to the possibility of a break-in. Sound boxes

(alarm bell boxes) should be installed so that they are not easily accessible to a burglar (i.e., higher than ten feet from the ground). Many devices include a second sound box inside the residence, usually at the basement level. Make certain that your alarm has a secondary power source option in case of a power failure.

- Other more elaborate systems involve a monitoring service which calls your residence and asks for a code word before automatically notifying the police. Quality systems can be expensive. Most also charge a monthly monitoring fee of about $30.00.
- Both systems may use a variety of detection components such as motion sensors, infra-red sensors, magnetic contacts for doors and windows, and glass breakage detectors. If you have a pet, you will need to inquire about which components will best suit your needs.
- Consider the installation of a panic button which automatically sounds the alarm when pressed. The buttons are installed in concealed locations throughout your residence. Some of the most common places are next to your bed, near your front door, and in a safe room.
- There are portable alarms that hang on doorknobs. If the door is opened the device will detect movement and sound a piercing ring. These devices are often used for travelling.

Entering Your Home

Here are some main guidelines to follow when entering your home.

- Have your keys in hand *before* getting to the front door.
- Be aware of people loitering on a street corner near your home.
- If you plan to return to your home after dark, leave an interior light on.
- Never enter the residence if the door is open, if there are other signs of forced entry, or if there is a suspicious car parked in your driveway. If this happens to you, go immediately to a safe area (i.e., a neighbours' house) and call the police.
- If you are asleep in the house and wake up during a burglary, pretend that you are still asleep. Do not attempt to confront the intruders. You may choose to leave the house if you can do so safely. You may choose to call 911 from your room. If this is the case you need not speak, as in most communities a police car will be dispatched to investigate a silent call.
- Make certain that the intruder has a clear escape route. If you position yourself as an obstacle between the intruder and his freedom, you could be putting yourself in harm's way.
- If you are attacked in your home, try to leave your residence and get help from a neighbour. It will be easier for you to leave than to attempt to make the aggressor leave.

Answering Your Door

If a stranger comes to your door do not pretend that you are not home. Often this is a screening technique that burglars use to select a home. They ring the doorbell and if no one answers they assume the house is unoccupied, and they break in, usually through a rear basement window. The proper response in this situation is to answer by talking through the door or a nearby window. Always keep the door locked. There is no reason good enough to warrant letting an unexpected stranger into your home. Do not allow little children to answer the door. They are quite likely to let anyone in. Be cautious about unannounced service people or delivery people, even if they provide identification. If you receive an unannounced service call, tell the person that you are busy and ask that he return at a later time (when others are home). If you request a service or repair man to your home you may wish to invite a neighbour, friend, or building superintendent over during the period that the worker is at your house. If this is not possible, and a service person begins to make you feel uncomfortable, wait outside of your residence for him to complete his work. Also, do not let anyone into your home on the pretext of helping with packages or anything else.

Be wary of some of the con types of approaches that assailants may use to gain entry into your home. Aside from posing as a repairman, aggressors may knock at your door claiming that they need you to let them make an emergency phone call for an ambulance. They may claim that there has been a terrible accident down the road. In such a situation you should not open your door to the stranger, but rather make the call for him. Sometimes police officers are impersonated to gain entrance into a victim's residence. Most honest, law-abiding citizens are not familiar with police officers. They have no idea what

an authentic badge or police uniform looks like. If you have the slightest doubt, do not hesitate to check it out by calling 911.

If you live alone you may want to create the illusion that someone else is home. One way this can be done is, as you approach the door to see who it is, you can say, 'I'll get it honey.' Installing a peephole and using it regularly is a good idea. Also, door chains are not as secure as most people think. They can be easily broken open with a kick or quick shoulder shove. Listing initials instead of first names is a good idea in telephone directories, mailboxes, address books, and cheques. Also consider having a roommate or a medium to large dog. If you are considering the purchase of a dog, you must realize that doing so requires a lifelong commitment to caring for your pet. Your dog does not have to have a mean temperament, he just needs to have a deep-sounding bark. In general, be very careful about the information that you give out to strangers at your front door, especially when you are alone at home. One rapist told of a incident back when he was seventeen years old:

Case Study: Alan
I had this part-time job after school. On my way to work I helped out my school by selling raffle tickets. As I went door-to-door with my sales pitch, I came to the door of an 11-year-old girl. I asked if I could speak to her parents. The girl told me that they were not home. I asked if I could speak to the babysitter, and she told me that she was home alone. I left the girl's house and went on to the next residence. There was no answer at this neighbouring

house. I thought about the situation. I had previously been fantasizing about raping a girl. I preferred younger victims because I thought they would be easier to control, more afraid, and less likely to tell. I went back to the girl's house, rang the doorbell, and asked if I could come in and wait for the girl's parents to arrive. The girl did not let me in at first. However, I fed her a line about how it was alright because everybody knows everybody in a small town. She felt pressured and did not want to look silly so she reluctantly let me in. I grabbed her by the arm and raped her at knife-point ... I know that if the girl would have said that her mother was upstairs sleeping or something like that, I would have never carried it out. (Anonymous offender, paraphrased)

Answering Your Telephone
Phone messages should state the number being called and that you are too busy to take the call. They should not reveal your name, nor the fact that you are not home. One suggestion is to have a male friend record the outgoing greeting message on your answering machine. A man's voice may help deter offenders who are seeking women who live alone. It is also wise to create the illusion that many people live at the residence. Always say, 'We can't come to the phone right now,' rather than, 'I can't come to the phone.'

When answering the telephone, never reveal to a stranger that you are home alone. Be cautious about answering telephone surveys that ask you for personal information. They are sometimes used as schemes whereby offenders attempt to learn more about potential victims in their process of selection.

The interviewer might be interested in whether you live alone, how old you are, and so on.

When responding to 'wrong number' calls, do not reveal your telephone number. Instead, ask the caller for the number he or she is attempting to reach. If you receive harassing phone calls, do not participate in any dialogue with the caller. Do not express anger, fear, or any other emotion. Simply hang up. If the calls persist disconnect the phone for an hour. If the caller is making death threats, or if you suspect the calls are associated to other criminal activity, notify the police, or see the section in this book on stalking. If the calls become repetitious, notify the police immediately. In most cases harassing calls are made by maladjusted individuals who view it as a game. However, there have been cases where stalkers begin to harass their victims in this way. Rapists and burglars sometimes resort to these tactics when selecting a potential victim. Your local telephone company may have several features to offer you for added security such as call trace, a pay per use service that immediately gives out the last number that called your residence. Call block can block out certain phone numbers from calling your line. Caller ID allows you to see the number of the caller before answering. However, modern technology also allows the calling party the option of suppressing their identity.

In Your Workplace
Potentially violent people in your workplace may include supervisors, colleagues, customers, ex-lovers, or friends. If someone in the workplace is the

victim of a stalking situation, the entire office staff is at risk of violence, and thus, appropriate measures should be taken. If a stalking situation is developing and affecting your workplace, see the section in this book on stalking. Co-workers under such conditions must be made aware of the threat. Any workplace that serves the public has a higher risk factor of workplace violence. High risk work environments usually involve health or social service agencies. Any government office to which the public has access can also be a likely target.

Behavior Associated with a Potentially Violent Person

While a potentially violent person may exhibit some noticeable traits, he or she may equally have a calm demeanour and give no direct indications of being violent. Some of the noticeable warning signs may include:

- Punching walls, damaging property, throwing objects
- Raised voice, yelling
- Arms crossed, fists clenched
- Mood swings
- Display of facial expression, red face, muscle tension
- Clenching or opening and closing hands

Your Response in a Crisis (De-escalation Strategies)

How you respond to a potentially violent situation may either aggravate or deter the situation. A violent episode can be difficult to determine or predict. One minute you may think everything is fine, the next minute the situation could be out of control. Do not attempt to reason with an aggressive person. You may start off by asking him or her to calm down once or twice. If you feel that the person is not able to listen or is out of control, ask if he or she would like to make an appointment to discuss the problem. If he or she refuses, demands to be dealt with on the spot, or simply ignores you, it will be necessary to get some assistance from co-workers or the police. The following are some helpful guidelines:

- Most importantly, never risk your personal safety to deal with an aggressive client.
- Stay calm and try not to be anxious. Notify the police if necessary.
- Show that you are genuinely concerned and that you are sincerely trying to help the person.
- Position yourself and the client in a place where others can see what is happening. Sitting is a less aggressive and less threatening position than standing.
- Ask the person what you can do for him or her, and what he or she expects. Try to understand what the individual expects from you, from the company, and the situation.
- Distinguish yourself from the company. For instance, make it clear to the aggressor that you are just an employee of the company, and you do not make the rules. Do not feel obligated to defend the company you are working for, or previous

decisions that you have made as an employee. Separate yourself from the situation or the rules if at all possible.

- Do not argue with, threaten, yell back at, or defend the company image with the aggressor. You do not want him to identify you as the source of the problem.
- Provide the aggressor with positive feedback without making promises that you cannot keep. For example: 'I'm glad we're having this discussion ...' 'I'll do what I can to help ...' Perhaps you can have the individual schedule an appointment for a later time.
- Keep a safe distance from the aggressor at all times. This should be a distance of about three feet.
- Do not touch the person.
- Do not wave your arms or fingers at the aggressor.
- Do not gang up on the person with the help of more than two employees if there has not yet been any physical confrontation. This may overwhelm the aggressor and cause a violent outburst if he or she interprets it as a threat.

Prevention Strategies

Here are some important prevention safety measures you can take:

- Adopt a zero tolerance policy on violence in your workplace.
- Remember that violence in the workplace can be caused by a co-worker just as easily as by a member of the public. Be aware of people who appear agitated.
- Avoid scheduling appointments with no one else in the area.
- Office design should have one main entrance to control access and maximize employee safety.
- Fire doors should be on an alarm system. At the very least, fire doors should be 'exit only doors' that automatically close when opened and otherwise remain in a locked position, not providing access into the building.
- All interior, office, and exterior doors should be numbered.
- Consideration should be given to installing office doors that have self-locking handles that open automatically from inside. All maintenance doors should be kept locked.
- For greater safety, offices that deal with the public should be, if possible, separated from offices that do not require public access.
- Ideally, work stations should be designed so that employees maintain visual contact with each other. Also, work stations should be designed so that if an aggressor is in front of your desk, he or she will not be blocking the doorway. Consider hiding places and escape routes out of your immediate work station.
- Sharp or blunt objects should be placed out of reach from the desk.
- If you feel you are in danger, excuse yourself and leave the area. Leave the building if you feel it necessary.
- Document all violent or threatening situations.

Your office should have a list of clients that may be violent. Special treatment may be required in these cases.

- Do not discuss company procedures outside the office.
- Be cautious about disclosing personal information to a client. Female hair stylists who serve male customers should be especially cautious about the information they are giving out. The nature of the job requires personable conversation. Just be cautious about giving out personal information.

The Emergency Code System

Imagine that you are sitting at your desk and the client you are dealing with begins to become violent or aggressive. A good method to employ in this sort of situation is to set up a code system known to all staff members. Every workplace should have a plan. Similar to a fire drill, employees should practise how to handle a violent episode. Companies that plan ahead through drills and mock role plays of violent episodes are much more likely to respond swiftly in a crisis situation.

The code system is usually based on a comment or message you leave with a colleague. For instance, it may be a phone message to your assistant stating your name and then a brief message such as, 'Cancel my appointment with Bob Smith.' When your assistant hears this message he or she will recognize that you are in an uncomfortable situation and will proceed by asking you a series of questions to which you will provide 'Yes' or 'No' responses. Your colleague may ask:

'Do you want a co-worker to help?'
'Do you want the police to help?'
'Are you being threatened?'
'Does the person have a weapon?'

Working after Hours

Here are some helpful guidelines:

- Try to refuse work on weekends or nights, especially if it means working alone. Many rapes occur during robberies. The robber selects the store because a woman is working alone.
- If you need to work alone after hours, lock the door to your office.
- Try not to be in the office alone. Perhaps there are other employees that need to put in some extra hours and you can arrange a common time with them. Another option may be to ask a friend to be with you while you work after hours. At the very least make sure that someone knows where you are.
- Keep lights around your work station turned on.
- Check all exits and entrances to make sure that they are secured.
- Notify building security of where you are working and ask that they check on you from time to time.
- Do not hesitate to ask security officers to escort you to your vehicle if your car is parked in a large empty company lot.

Establishing Boundaries with Co-Workers

- Do not engage in conversations that make you feel uncomfortable. Excuse yourself and walk away, or state to your co-worker that you are not comfortable talking about a certain topic.

- Be cautious about how much information you reveal about your personal life at work, especially with co-workers who appear overly friendly. You have the right to keep personal information private.
- If a particular individual in your work environment alarms you, discuss your concerns with other co-workers. It is common that aggressors usually target more than one person.

IN YOUR CAR

Parking Your Car
Here are some suggestions:

- Try to park your car in a well-lit, busy area.
- When parking in more secluded places, make sure to look around before getting out of your vehicle.
- Do not leave your car in parking lots where attendants leave vehicle doors unlocked or request to hold your keys. If you must, leave only your ignition key. This guideline is also useful when leaving your car for servicing at a garage.
- Ask the parking attendant whether the lot will still be attended to and well-lit when you return.
- When parking in large underground or enclosed lots be extra cautious of the surroundings. Walk in the centre aisles rather than between the parked cars. If you have the choice, park in lots that have security patrols or an attendant. Areas that have heavy pedestrian or vehicle traffic would also be preferred.

- When parking in any type of lot, try to park close to a walkway or building entrance. Always avoid parking far away from others.
- Try to remember the level and section number that you parked in.
- Be aware of your environment before exiting your vehicle. Turn off your engine, listen for any sounds. Use your mirrors to help scan the area.

Returning to Your Car
Some important points to remember:

- Upon approaching your vehicle be aware of your surroundings. The best possible situation is if you can clearly see your vehicle from a safe distance. Are there any obstructions that are limiting your view?
- Check under the vehicle from a distance to make sure that no one is hiding under your car. As you move closer, be alert to other vehicles parked close by.
- Suspicious situations would include: an occupied vehicle parked close by, or a nearby vehicle in which you cannot see inside (e.g., a van or a sedan with black tinted windows). Also, be cautious of any suspicious person approaching you as you near your car.
- If there is a group of individuals near your car: do not attempt to approach your car, immediately contact the police or a security officer for an escort.
- If your car looks odd, or perhaps has a flat tire, leave at once and seek help.
- Visually check the front and rear passenger com-

partments before entering. If you own a hatch-back check the rear compartment as well.

- Have your key in your hand *before* reaching your car. Many women become victimized at their car door when they are unsuspectingly caught off guard as they fumble through their purses for the car keys.
- Consider installing a remore car starter. As you approach your vehicle in a parking lot, activate the signal to start your car. Many car starters illuminate the parking lights as they start. During the evening hours, this may deter an aggressor who might think that there is someone else in the car waiting for you.
- If your instincts tell you that something is not right, leave the situation immediately and request an escort from building security, a store manager, or contact the police. Ignoring your instincts if you do not feel safe is simply not worth the risk.

While Driving

- Keep your car in good running condition. Make it a habit of always keeping your gas tank at least half full.
- Try to plan out the route that you will take ahead of time. This includes knowing where you may be able to stop in case of an emergency. You should be familiar with public pay phones and businesses that stay open late on your route.
- Do not stop for vehicles in distress. Inform the nearest police officer of disabled cars. You may choose to contact the police by calling 911 on your cellular phone. There is usually no charge for the call and you will be familiarizing yourself with the service in case of emergency.
- Keep your doors locked when in the vehicle. If you must keep a window open, it should be the driver's window. When driving on city streets your windows should be rolled up no less than three-quarters of the way. You should always drive in the lane furthest from the curb when possible.
- Be alert for vehicles that appear to be following you. If you suspect you are being followed, do not drive home; rather, drive to a police station, fire station, hospital emergency room, large hotel, or any other busy area where you can safely call the police. If this option is not possible honk your horn and turn on your emergency flashers; try to get the licence plate number of the car following you.
- Keep valuables such as wallets and purses out of sight, rather than on the seat next to you.
- Varying your drive to work (leaving at a different times or using a different route) makes it much more difficult for someone to predict your actions. Research suggests that most stranger offenders plan their assaults by learning about their victim's patterns.
- You are much less at risk if others are in the car with you. Consider car-pooling options whenever possible.
- Always have the financial resources necessary in case of an emergency. This would include bus or cab fare and some change to call home. If your daughter is old enough to drive, and you trust

her with the family car, then perhaps she would be equally responsible with her own credit card and cellular phone that she can resort to in case of emergency. At the very least, parents who allow their children to drive alone should provide them with a basic calling card (some phone cards have fixed limits). This would allow their children to call home free of charge.

- Do not stop if someone signals that there is something is wrong with your car. Drive to a safe, busy, well-lit location.
- If you are being stopped by an unmarked police car and you feel that you have not done anything wrong, consider your situation. Are you alone at night in a secluded area, or are you car-pooling home from work during the rush hour? The action that you should take depends on the situation. If the person attempting to pull you over is in an unmarked police car, and if you are alone at night in a secluded area, you may choose to stop your vehicle. Remain in the car with your doors and windows locked and closed. When the officer approaches explain to him that you would like to drive to a safer (busy, well-lit) location. If you have any doubt ask that the officer have a uniform patrol car dispatched to your location. Do not feel guilty about making such a request. If you have a cellular phone you may choose to contact 911 for verification. Do not be quick to exit your vehicle. No matter how demanding the request, follow your instincts.
- Try not to pull up too close to cars at stop lights. Leave room to get out in case of an emergency. If you cannot pull out, blow your horn until help arrives or you can move your vehicle.
- If someone tries to force you off the road, keep your engine running and the car in gear. As soon as he gets out of his car, drive away. Do not exit your vehicle.
- If someone forces his way into your car, stop the car, take the keys if you can, and jump out.
- When driving a friend home or to her car, make sure that she is safely in her home or that her car has started, before driving away. Ask friends to do the same for you.
- If you are driving home, have your house keys ready before you exit your car.

If Your Car Breaks Down

- If possible stop on a busy and well-lit street.
- Put on your four-way emergency flashers. If you break down on the highway, you may want to light some flares as well.
- Ideally, wait for assistance inside your locked vehicle with the windows rolled up.
- If you are in a secluded place, stay in your car with the windows rolled up. If someone stops to help, talk through the window or lower it no more than one inch. Tell him that he is the second person who stopped, and ask him if he could call the police for you, just in case the first person forgot. This little technique will create doubt in a potential offender. He will not be able to know if help will arrive at any moment and will most likely be deterred. However, chances are that this

individual is really just trying to help and will call help for you as requested.

- If you find yourself in a situation where someone is insisting that he can fix your car, be cautious. Tell him that you would rather have your regular garage look at the problem. Ask him to call for assistance instead. If he persists be cautious and trust your instincts; it may seem like a nice gesture on his part, but it also means that he is not listening to you. Do not get out of your car. If the person becomes aggressive or hostile, remain in the vehicle and sound the horn. Depending on the nature of the breakdown you may even be able to drive away. For instance, it is much safer to drive on a flat tire until you reach a safe, well-lit, busy area before stopping to change your tire. This may cause tire damage, but it is the safest option.
- You may choose to place a 'call police' sign in your back window. Many automotive stores sell decorative dashboard sun shades that have the 'call police' message printed on its backside.
- Never stop to assist a stranded motorist on the roadside. If you want to help you can always drive to a busy area and call the police from a safe location to report the situation.

An aggressor may choose to disguise himself as a good Samaritan or a police officer to attempt to gain your trust. Mary was eighteen years old when a man claiming to be a mall security officer approached her while she was shopping in a department store in a small New England town:

Case Study: Mary

He asked if I was the owner of a red Chevrolet, startled, I replied 'Yes.' The man knew this information because he was probably scouting out the parking area for a single woman and saw me drive in. He went on to explain how someone had vandalized my car, and how he needed me to accompany him to the car to make out an incident report. Once we reached the car, I found a broken headlight probably caused by the offender. The man started making me feel really uneasy. He seemed very nervous and seemed to be constantly watching other people as they passed by. My instincts told me something about him was not right. I told him that I would call the police and make a report. I made sure to keep a good distance from him. I went back into the store and the manager informed me that the store does not have a security officer. When the police arrived, they informed me that there have been similar incidents in neighbouring towns involving a male impersonating a security officer and a police officer.

In an Accident

- Stay in your vehicle providing there is no risk of fire or explosion
- If your vehicle is operational, ask that the other driver follow you to a busier location. If your vehicle is disabled, stay in the car, providing there is no risk of fire or explosion. Keep your windows rolled up and your doors locked. You can exchange information with the other driver by rolling your window down about one inch. If the driver is hostile and people are close by, you may want to honk your horn to draw their attention. If

your car is not disabled, you may choose to leave the scene and notify the police from a safer location. Although it is illegal to leave the scene of an accident, most courts would find it reasonable to do so in order to notify the police, especially in the case where a woman is alone and in fear for her own safety. However, you may have to explain these actions in court. Sometimes an aggressor can manipulate his target into getting out of her vehicle in a secluded area, such as in an incident which happened to Ashley.

Case Study: Ashley

I was returning from my evening shift where I work as a nursing assistant at a major hospital centre. I had been working the evening shift all week. I left the hospital parking lot at about 11:30 that night and began to drive home. It is only a fifteen-minute ride from the hospital to my front door. On my route, I travel through quiet residential streets. I never suspected that anything bad could happen to me in such an upscale community. I recall stopping my vehicle at a four-way intersection. This intersection is usually very busy during the day, so the city installed a four-way flashing red light so that traffic in all directions stops. As I made my stop, the vehicle behind mine bumped into my rear bumper. At that moment all that I could think about was getting out of my car to inspect the damage. I even opened my car door and put one foot on the road before I started to realize how strange this situation was. I began to think to myself, here I am in the middle of this intersection alone with someone and there is no one else around. I just realized how different this neighbourhood was at night. I realized that I was totally se-

cluded. I think my instincts told me that something was wrong as I began to get out of my car. The driver of the other car appeared to be waiting to see if I would get out of my vehicle first. I got back in the car and locked the doors. The driver never got out of his car: He backed up and drove away. I drove to a gas station that was still open and inspected my car for damage and called the police. The officer that arrived to take the report told me that there was a man in the area who has been creating minor traffic accidents to lure his victims out their cars to sexually assault them. I was really glad that I followed my instincts.

Asking for Directions

If you are lost, try to ask for directions at a police station or a fire station. If this is not possible try a service station or a restaurant. Try to ask directions so that others will not overhear your conversation and learn that you are a tourist or lost. Never ask for directions from people on the street.

Other Important Points about Car Safety

- Select a reliable service station for car repairs. Try to make it a habit to visit the same garage.
- One of the easiest ways to disable a car is to taint its fuel. Adding water in a fuel tank that is less than half full will produce a stalling effect. Adding a significant amount of sugar or sand will cause the engine to seize. Consider using a locking fuel cap. These can be purchased from many automobile accessory shops or at your original dealership. Many Japanese car makers have this as a standard feature on most models.

- If you plan on selling your car privately through an ad in the paper, have a male friend handle the calls. If possible have the male go on test rides with prospective buyers, rather than yourself.
- Consider the purchase of a cellular phone.
- Never pick up hitchhikers.

IN PUBLIC PLACES

Using Public Transit

There are many cases involving assaultive behaviour that occurs on public transit. Take, for instance, the case of a fourteen-year-old girl in Ottawa, Ontario, who was sexually molested in the middle of a crowded city bus during rush hour. The aggressor sat beside her, trapping the girl into the window seat. He convincingly told the young girl that he had a knife in his coat pocket and that if she made a sound, he would kill her. The girl was terrified as the man fondled her for over twenty minutes. After speaking with her parents about what had happened, the girl decided to report the incident to the police.

In a prominent Montreal suburb a similar incident was reported to the police. An eighteen-year-old college student was on her way home from a class late one Wednesday evening. She boarded a city bus at a busy downtown stop with two intoxicated males who seemed to be acting oddly. Once on the bus, she sat about mid-way between the front and rear. The two males began harassing her by making graphic sexual comments. The girl remembers that the two males attracted the attention of most of the thirty or so passengers during her twenty-minute ride into the suburbs:

Case Study: Laura

People knew that these jerks were bothering me, but they did not help me. No one wanted to get involved. They started off by making comments such as, 'Hey baby wanna party … wanna play with me?' I did my best to just ignore them. Everyone in the bus seemed to be scared of them, because no one did anything. People just let it happen. As the bus emptied, I began to wonder what I was going to do. The two men were drunk and seemed to be getting louder and louder. Soon they moved closer to me. One was standing right on the side of me, while the other was sitting in the seat in front of me. They started to play with my hair. One of the guys ripped open a condom package and pushed the condom in my face. The other man poured beer over me and began to lick it off my neck. I felt completely out of control. The bus driver did absolutely nothing as he continued driving on his route. I think he was too afraid to intervene, but probably pretended not to notice. I simply froze and began to cry … I couldn't even scream or yell for help. I was too afraid to respond. I think I froze because I never thought that something so horrible could happen to me. I never thought that I could be victimized by something like that in my neighbourhood. I know now that it could happen to anyone anywhere and at anytime. It has taken me a long time to come to terms with what happened that evening. I think if something like this would ever happen again, I would be able to fight back and protect myself. I have thought about that situation a million times. I realize that it can happen to me and I have developed a plan in case something like that ever happens to me again.

We would all like to believe that we could count on the goodness of others to automatically and instinctively come to our aid in time of need. However, sometimes people have an instinct to not get involved even in a group situation such as the one mentioned above. A strategy that might work in this situation is to directly request the help of one person, rather than simply addressing the group. The following tips will help you reduce your chances of being victimized:

- Always try to sit near the driver; avoid the rear of the bus when it is not heavily occupied.
- Avoid sitting in window seats when you are alone.
- Make it a habit to arrive just before the bus, thereby limiting the time you spend waiting at the stop.
- Use busier stops when possible, rather than deserted ones.
- Do not sleep on the bus; always be aware of your environment.
- If someone makes you feel uncomfortable, change seats or move away.
- If someone harasses you, draw public attention to the situation by yelling out that someone is bothering you. Do not be afraid to cause a scene or to tell the driver. Few people realize that the driver has the responsibility of keeping order on the bus.
- If you feel that you are being followed, tell the driver and ask that she or he lets you off at a busy place or open business between stops. Some transit companies have policies whereby women can ask to be dropped of between stops during night and weekend service.
- Never get off at a secluded stop if you think you are being followed.
- Trust your instincts. If you feel uncomfortable after getting off the bus, walk immediately to a place where there are other people.
- On subways, during quiet traffic hours, try to sit in the first car, right near the driver's door.
- Do not display jewelry. Turn rings around so the stones are on the palm side of your hand; hide necklaces inside sweaters.
- Plan out your route in advance. Know how to get where you are going, and know how to get back.

Elevators and Stairs

- Stairwells that are fireproof are also soundproof. The elevator is a better option than fire stairs.
- It may be difficult to position and balance yourself on stairs in the case of an altercation.
- In an elevator, stand next to the control panel, but do not turn your back on the other passengers.
- Do not get on the elevator with only one other person. If you are in an elevator and someone suspicious enters, get off immediately or at the next floor.
- If an incident arises, do not press the alarm button. This can actually stop the elevator, trapping you with the assailant. Push as many floor buttons as you can. This will create a multitude of

opportunities to escape or attract attention to the fact that you need help.

On the Street

- When carrying bags or parcels always keep one hand free.
- Keep your wallet in your coat pocket and avoid carrying a purse. If you must carry a purse, do not place the purse strap around your neck. Many victims are injured by purse-snatchers who end up pulling their victim to the ground in their attempt to steal the purse. Carry the purse slightly in front of you with one hand on it. The strap should be over your shoulder, not your neck.
- Keep some money out of your wallet, perhaps in a coat pocket, in case of emergency.
- Wear loose-fitting clothes and flat shoes. Be aware of how you can or cannot move in the clothes you are wearing.
- Walk near the curb of the sidewalk, unless a car approaches.
- Avoid wearing headphones, reading, or wearing sunglasses. These items can impair your awareness about your surroundings.
- Avoid secluded areas or shortcuts. Stay on busy, well-lit streets.
- Walk or jog *against* the traffic.
- Ignore harassing comments.
- When possible, walk around groups of men, rather than through them. Consider crossing the street if necessary to avoid such a group.
- As you approach the front door of your home,

have your house key ready in your hand, especially if no one else is home.

Ellen, a thirty-five-year-old social worker from Montreal, was waiting for a friend on a downtown street corner when a man approached her:

Case Study: Ellen
'Can you tell me how to get to the subway station?' the man had asked. Initially, I was relieved that that was all he wanted from me. As I began to explain to him the directions, I realized that he was not really listening to what I was telling him. He began to move closer to me, and then he asked me who I was waiting for and what I was doing here. I was really caught off guard. Here was this guy who was polite and attractive. Suddenly he was really close to me. I took two steps back and said to him, 'Leave me alone!'

Ellen's aggressor did leave her alone. He might have been gauging her awareness level or evaluating whether she was suspicious or afraid of him. If he could distract her with a question and position himself close to her, it was likely that he would have continued to attempt his assault. Reacting at the initial stages could dissuade the offender into choosing a less suspecting individual. Try to answer strangers with negative responses (e.g., 'No ... I do not have the time,' 'No ... I do not know where Main Street is,' 'No ... I do not know how to get to Main Street') and limit the amount of dialogue in situations where you feel vulnerable or uncomfortable.

If You Are Being Followed

- Never go home. You do not want the offender to find out where you live.
- If you feel that you are being followed, turn around and look at the offender. This is an assertive move that will let him know that you are aware of his presence, and he will not be able to surprise you. Assertively instruct him to stop following you.
- If you are being followed, cross the street and change directions. If the offender persists, and you are on a busy street, address him loudly. Tell him to stop following you. Your goal is to make everyone in the area aware of your situation. Another option would be to go into an open business and call the police. If you are in a secluded area you could attempt to break a store window or knock on the door of a residence that appears occupied. You may also try to set off car alarms by bumping into or kicking expensive-looking automobiles in your path. In a situation where you are on a secluded residential street during the evening hours and fear for your safety, consider throwing a rock through a window of a house that seems occupied. Often people do not want to get involved in other people's problems. However, breaking someone's window makes it their problem as well. Even though you will have replace the window and explain your actions to authorities, overall it may be a wise move.
- If you choose to run, remember that you need to have a place to run to. You will have to address the pros and cons: perhaps it may depend upon how far away he is from you, or upon this distance to your destination. You have to feel confident that you can reach that destination before the offender reaches you. Males, on average, are usually faster than females. If he catches up, you will be at a disadvantage since you will have your back turned to your assailant at the point of confrontation (see physical resistance).
- Remember that is always easier to fight back on the street than once you have been pulled into a car.

Biking, Jogging, or Other Outdoor Activities

- Vary your route and time so that your actions are not predictable.
- Consider bringing a friend or a dog along.
- Choose a route that appears safe and well-populated.
- Avoid doing outdoor activities alone at night.
- Know open businesses and other areas that you can go to for help.
- Be wary around restrooms in public places. Check all the stalls, but use the one closest to the exit.

At Automated Teller Banking Machines

- Use busy, well-lit locations that have an unobstructed view from the street. The best options are those located in convenience stores or supermarkets. Some progressive cities have begun to put ATMs in police station lobbies. If this is not the case in your community, mention the idea to police authorities.

- Consider using a drive-up ATM rather than a walk-up. You are safer in your locked vehicle at the drive-up ATM.
- Consider bringing a friend along for company and security.
- Always take your transaction slip, as this slip usually indicates the balance of funds left in your account. Immediately put your money away, do not count it in front of others.
- If you are approached by a robber, do not resist. Give him or her the money or whatever other material possessions that he or she wants. As you hand over the goods, try to use that very moment as an opportunity to escape. Your goal is to shorten the amount of time spent in that situation. As you escape you may choose to yell and scream as you run to a busy area. Leave the offender as soon as possible and report the incident to the police. It is generally not a good idea to leave the primary crime scene with the offender, under any circumstance, since the secondary site that he or she will bring you to will be a much more controlled environment with fewer chances for you to escape or summon help.

Hitchhiking

- Avoid hitchhiking.
- In an emergency, flag down a police car or call your local police department and explain the situation.
- Teenagers especially may find it more difficult to

avoid the temptation to hitchhike. If you choose to hitchhike try to have a friend with you.

- Try not to hitchhike at night.
- Do not accept rides from people who have changed directions to pick you up.
- Do not accept rides from people driving vehicles such as panel trucks or mini-vans, as you would not be able to tell how many people were in the rear of the vehicle.
- Do not accept rides from a vehicle occupied by more than one male. Your safest option would be riding with another female.
- Ask the driver where he is going before giving your destination.
- If you have a male friend with you, let him get in the car first. Motorists have driven off with female hitchhikers before their male companion could enter the vehicle.
- Get the licence number of the vehicle before you get in.
- Make certain that the inside door latch-release works before entering the vehicle, and try to keep the window rolled down.
- As you enter the vehicle scan the entire passenger compartment. If anything seems odd, do not get in.
- Be prepared to get out of the car if the driver wants to make a detour or an unscheduled stop.
- Keep the conversation impersonal and do not mention that you have money.

TRAVEL SAFETY

Rental Cars
Do not rent from rental car companies that display

their name anywhere on the exterior of the vehicle. A rent-a-car bumper sticker on your vehicle serves as a clear indicator that you are a tourist or visitor to the area. Most companies no longer place such stickers. Consider bringing your cellular phone on the trip. Contact your provider to ensure that your phone will function in the region. Many of the larger rental car agencies in the United States also rent cell phones to their customers. Remember to call 911 to report stranded motorists or accidents, as this will serve as a test call in case you need their help.

Taxis

Make a note of the company and cab number before getting in the cab. If your instincts tell you that something is not right, and the cab is at a halt, do not hesitate to get out. If the car is moving, make up an excuse (e.g., you are feeling sick and are about to vomit) to get out in a well-populated area.

Hotels

- Choose hotels that have a twenty-four-hour front desk service.
- Hotels should have room phones in case you need to reach the front desk in an emergency. Use the phone to call the front desk to ensure that it works properly.
- Choose hotels in which the doors to the rooms open from an interior hall, rather than directly from a parking lot. This makes it more difficult for others to know your exact room.
- Avoid motels that have two room entrances. Usu-

ally these motels will have one hall entrance and one parking lot entrance.
- Second-floor rooms are generally safer than those on the first floor.
- Electronic card keys are the most secure and tend to be found in the more expensive lodging options. Room keys that have the name and address and room number of the hotel that you are staying at are dangerous, especially if you lose the key. Most hotels now give out a key with the room number indicated on it, but not the hotel name or address. Keep in mind that there are probably several missing keys for your room. Also, anyone working at the hotel is likely to have the opportunity to gain access to your room when you are not in it.
- Check your room thoroughly every time you return to it. Have a hotel staff member show you to your room initially. Check behind the drapes, in the bathroom, and under the bed. Make sure that the windows are locked. If a window is not able to be secured properly, refuse to stay in that room.
- Always stay at hotels that have an additional deadbolt lock and bar lock on the door. Always use these locks. One of the victims who was interviewed told about what happened to her when she stayed at a well-known discount motel near the airport of a big city on a business trip.

Case Study: Linda
I went to sleep only to awaken a few hours later with some strange man on top of me. When I resisted, the light on the bedside table was sent crashing to the floor, causing the assailant to run away. I immediately notified the

police. It wasn't long before the detectives traced the incident to the front desk clerk. His friend had seen me check in alone. Later that evening he bought a duplicate room key from his friend for five dollars and let himself into the room. Unfortunately, I had forgotten to use the other deadbolt lock on the door. (Anonymous victim, paraphrased)

- For added safety you may choose to prop a chair against the door on an angle, or place a rubber door stop under the door. It is very difficult for someone to gain access without making noise if this is done properly.
- You may chose to purchase a personal safety travel alarm. This type of device senses motion so that if someone enters your room, the alarm will sound. This type of alarm can be purchased at most department stores, electronics stores, or alarm service agencies.
- Register at the front desk with a first initial rather than full first name.
- Ask that hotel staff keep your room number confidential when taking messages.
- Upon checking in ask that the staff not announce your room number if others are loitering around the area. Ask them to write it down on a piece of paper and hand it to you.
- Verify the credentials of any unexpected service people with the front desk.
- Be sure that the bathroom shower curtain is only drawn when it is being used, as it provides an excellent hiding place.
- When you leave your hotel room and plan to return in the evening, leave a light on, leave the television on at a normal volume, and make certain to draw the window shades. This gives the impression that someone is in the room.
- Upon entering your hotel room, if your instincts suggest something is strange or unsafe, act on your instincts. Go immediately to the front desk of the hotel and ask for an escort to your room.

Other Important Points

- When travelling to a foreign country learn as much as you can about the culture and laws of the region.
- Dress casually when possible. If you have a camera hanging around your neck, you are likely to stand out as a tourist.
- When travelling to a country that requires you to have your passport, make a photocopy of it. This sometimes makes it easier to get a replacement.
- Always try to travel with a friend.
- Be cautious not to disclose personal information to other travellers.

OTHER SAFETY TIPS

Answering and Placing Classified Ads
Whether you are selling used furniture, looking for a mate, or job hunting, you will need to exercise caution in answering and placing classified ads. Many women are sexually assaulted by men who use telephone party lines, matchmaking services, and dating lines as a stalking ground for their victims.

If you are selling household items through a classified advertisement in the local paper, do not list a female name as a the contact person. Also, do not list your address in the ad. Have the person call you first and only give out your address when the potential buyer has committed to making an appointment to see the item. When the potential buyer visits your residence, do not let him see more of your home than he has to. Do not give out unnecessary personal information. If you are buying an item through such an ad, make certain to have a friend with you if it involves visiting a strange address.

Female real estate agents need to be especially careful in situations where they are accompanying a potential male home buyer to an unoccupied house. Learn what you can about the situation of the home before meeting your client. Have your office keep a special file on abandoned homes in the neighbourhood. Exercising caution in such a situation may mean using the buddy system. Bring along a co-worker to the site as a safe measure.

Classified advertisements that offer employment provide another opportunity for an assailant to lure his victim into a dangerous situation. Ads for modelling agencies or acting classes are high risk and deserve to be approached with caution. However, even regular job ads can be used to mislead honest people in search of work. One of the inmates interviewed tells how he used this approach:

Case Study: Kevin
I would place an ad in the local paper looking for a babysitter displaying a good hourly rate. I would not use my real name or address. In the ad, I would list the address of an apartment building across the street from my place as my address, but I would put a random apartment number and not give my phone number. People, mostly young college or high school girls would send me their resume. The mail would be left in the lobby of the apartment building since it was not addressed to a specific apartment. The postal worker usually left the mail in the apartment lobby thinking that the right person would find it. Sometimes I would even check the mail before the tenants had a chance to, removing the resumes addressed to my fake name on my own. I really had no trouble with this system. I would have many phone numbers and addresses of young girls. Sometimes I would go by their house to see what they looked like. Sometimes I would follow them to see what they were up to. I knew I could have any one of them. It was just too easy. I would call them from a pay phone about three weeks after receiving their letter or resume. I waited this long because I knew they probably had sent out many resumes and would have forgotten about my tiny ad by this time. I would sound all professional and ask them about their skills and studies. Then I would set up an interview with them telling them to meet me somewhere. (Anonymous offender, paraphrased)

Exercise caution when searching for jobs. Do not be afraid to ask the employer details about the company or himself prior to meeting. If possible find out ahead of time where the employer is. Schools and community organizations that run employment services should have a screening procedure to verify job advertisements. A specially designated room that can be used for potential employers to interview potential employees on site at schools would also be a good safeguard. If you are in doubt about an employer, bring a friend to the interview.

IN YOUR RELATIONSHIPS

Meeting Someone New

It is always easier to meet someone new when there are common friends involved. However, sometimes this is not the case. When meeting someone new, be cautious about how much and what information you disclose about yourself. Do not give out your phone number right away, ask for his instead. Try to learn as much as you can about him: where he lives, where he works, and what he does for leisure. This should come up casually in conversation. At the same time, try not to be too specific about your own situation, that is, where you live and work. If you have common friends, try to find out how he treated his previous dates. Most offenders turn out to be repeat offenders and have a history of abusing victims. They have certain negative attitudes and beliefs concerning women and sex. These negative attitudes are likely to be reflected in how they have interacted with other women in their past.

Awareness Strategies to Reduce Date Rape

Tell People Where You Will Be. Make it a habit to inform a friend, sibling, or parent where you are going, with whom, and also when you expect to return from the date.

Set and Communicate Your Limits Clearly. It is crucial that sexual limits are set at an early stage of the relationship. These limits should be expressed clearly to remove all doubt from your date's mind. It is best to be up front and direct with the date. A creative yet less effective way to communicate your limits to your date is to talk to him about a particular situation. This may involve creating a fictional situation that you can make up concerning a friend's boyfriend. Your story should reflect how upset you were to find out what her date had tried to do. For example: 'I cannot believe Kim's boyfriend. Yesterday he thought he could sleep with her because she let him buy her dinner ... I cannot believe him; he is so disrespectful towards her. I am so glad I have you because I know you would never try anything like that.' You can then perhaps address your own concerns: 'At this point in our relationship I am definitely not ready for a sexual commitment.'

Be careful that your date does not misread any subconscious messages that you may be sending. Saying 'no' always means 'no.' However, there is an alarmingly large portion of males that seem to have a problem understanding the concept of 'no.' It is not a woman's obligation to educate men on the concept of 'no.' Furthermore, it is not a women's obligation to prevent being raped. This is a crime that can only be placed on the aggressor. It is unfortunate and unfair that women have to use such strategies to reduce the risk of being victimized by acquaintance rape in our society. One of these strategies is to send a very clear message, so clear that the aggressor can in no way think that 'no' means something other than 'no.' For instance, saying 'no' in joking manner, rather than in a serious tone, may confuse a male who has trouble reading your limits. In one study (Muehlenhard and Linton, 1987), male aggressors reported that they often felt led on by their dates. Female victims reported that the male thought they had been led on. Males seemed to have a positive response to females who gave them direct and clear limits. This resulted in having positive consequences on the relationship (ibid.). If there is confusion or ambiguity, clarify it verbally. You are the best person to decide what is right and wrong for you. Acting on how you feel is usually the right thing to do.

If you are victimized by an acquaintance always remember that it is not your fault. The aggressor is responsible for his actions. You could follow all of the prevention strategies listed in this book, and it could still happen to you. The overall goal is simply to help reduce your risk of attack.

Examples of unclear and clear communication options

– She says: 'No, not right now; I have a headache.'
– He thinks: 'Okay, I can wait till she feels better.'
– A clear alternative: 'Look, I do not want you to do that, and if you continue it is called rape!'

– She says: 'No not right now, okay?'
– He thinks: 'How about later?' or 'No, it is not all right and if I pressure her a bit more she will change her mind.'

– A clear alternative: 'I like it when you touch my breasts, but don't touch me down there.'

– She says: 'I really like you, but I am not sure we should go any farther.' (She means stop, you are going too fast.)
– He thinks: 'All I have to do is convince her. Besides she really likes me.'
– A clear alternative: 'Please don't do that.'

– She says laughingly: 'Come on, stop that.' (She means I am not comfortable doing this, stop right now.)
– He thinks: 'She is just playing around, she is not really serious.'
– A clear alternative: 'I am serious. Stop that right now!'

– She says: 'Do you really think that this is a good idea?' (She means I am not comfortable doing this.)
– He thinks: 'She is leaving this up to me, so I have to take charge.'
– A clear alternative: 'I really like kissing you, but I don't want you to touch me there.'

– She says: 'Gee, I don't know.' (She means I am not comfortable doing this.)
– He thinks: 'Maybe? This means I will have to be more persistent and reassure her.'
– A clear alternative: 'I really like when you kiss me, but I don't want to go any further.'

It is always best to communicate limits clearly in dating relationships. Statements that are simple and polite reduce the likelihood of misunderstanding. Some of the alternative statements listed above provide simple clear 'no' messages, while others communicate to the date what is acceptable behaviour and that which is not. It may be necessary to repeat a statement to the date if he is not intent on listening. The repeated version should be even more assertively stated. Perhaps the words 'Listen to me' or 'You are not listening to me' should be stressed. Remember to back up your words with actions and body language that supports your message. Saying 'no' while laughing will not be as effective as if 'no' is said with a serious tone backed by body language such as pushing an aggressor's hand away.

Feel Good about Yourself

Women with a low level of self-worth are more likely to be victimized by an attack. Women who realize that they have a right to demand respect from their dates are better able to avoid an assault because they know that they are worth fighting for. Women who are proud and confident in life demand respect from their dates.

Be Involved in Decision Making

Be involved in the actual planning of the date before it begins. Make certain that it is a joint effort, rather than letting your date making all the decisions. For instance, be certain that you are doing something you both agree on (e.g., watching a movie), rather than feeling forced or pressured to do solely what he wants to do.

Do Not Go Alone

Single dates should take place in public, especially for the first few times. Arrange to have another couple of your choice (not his) double-date, or meet him in a public place. Concerts, movies, or sporting events are good choices that provide a more public environment. First dates and casual dates are associated with a higher risk (Browder, 1985). Keep in mind that most date rapes occur in isolated areas. Some of the more common environments include an upstairs bedroom during a house party, in a parked car, and any other convenient place that two people might want to go for privacy (Muehlenhard and Linton, 1987).

Be Independent

Exercise your own independence. Do not accept an offer of transportation to and from the event with your date. Arrange to meet him at the site and have someone pick you up if necessary. It is very important that you do not put yourself in a situation where you are depending on him for anything. This includes the expenses incurred on the date. If he wants to pay for the movie, insist on paying for supper afterward. It may be a good idea to plan a date that does not require money. Always have enough money to take a cab home, or at least enough to call someone who can pick you up.

Stay Sober

Heavy alcohol and drug consumption by the victim and offender are a common risk factor in date rape cases (Muehlenhard and Linton, 1987; Brozan, 1986). Nearly 75 per cent of males and 55 per cent of females had been drinking or taking drugs just before the assault occurred (Warshaw, 1988). For instance, Campus Police at the University of California at Los Angeles reported that all acquaintance rapes that occurred on campus were alcohol-related (Citrano, 1994). Staying sober helps you stay in control of yourself. Drugs and alcohol will severely impair your ability to recognize warning signs leading to an assault. If the man is also drinking, it will also have adverse effects on him which may result in a loss of good judgment. If possible, try to avoid environments where heavy drinking is the main event.

We can stress that individuals abstain from using drugs and drinking alcohol, but these substances have an entrenched presence, especially in the college party environment. It is important to remember that if you do decide to drink, do so responsibly. If you are at a party, do not rely upon others to take care of you. Always try to stay in control. As an added precaution, when you go to parties use the buddy system. Plan to keep watch over each other's behaviour beforehand. If your buddy seems intoxicated, it may be the cue for both of you to leave the party.

Trust Your Instincts and Be Assertive

All the victims interviewed mentioned that there was some point during the date when they felt something was not right. Their instincts warned them of a possibly dangerous situation. However, the women did not act on their instincts for two main reasons. First, they liked their dates and did not want to look silly or be embarrassed for overreacting to his ag-gressive approach. Second, they often did not feel comfortable being 'up-front' because they thought they would hurt the other person's feelings. These women found that their situations worsened to a point where they lost all sense of control. It is important not to ignore warning signs. Identify and stay away from males who choose not to listen to and ignore clear messages that are sent to them concerning the woman's feelings and limits. If you are ever in a situation that makes you feel uncomfortable, listen to your instincts and try to get out of it as soon as possible. It is better to have an embarrassing moment than to be scarred by a the trauma of a sexual assault. Listening to your instincts is of utmost importance and cannot be stressed enough. Remember, if something does not seem right, it probably is not. Most of us have instincts that are far more accurate than we think. If your instincts tell you something does not seem right, end the evening earlier than you had anticipated.

Watch Out for Male Peer Pressure

Avoid being with your date in places where there are an overwhelming number of males, especially environments that contain a great deal of male peer pressure. This type of place may include team parties, fraternity clubs, or male dormitory residences on college campuses. It would be wise to exercise caution any time the number of males greatly outnumbers the number of females in any party situation.

Watch Out for an Overly Friendly Date

A common characteristic of many aggressors in date

rape cases is that they are moving much too quickly towards intimacy. Many victims claimed that they found their dates being overly friendly, or simply *coming on* too strong and lacking the ability to recognize their date's subtle messages to slow down. If a woman feels uncomfortable that her boundaries are being violated, she should tell the aggressor in a clear statement that his behaviour is not acceptable. This is important since *personal boundary violation is one of the most reliable warning signs of an impeding assault*. Acting on instincts is crucial in date rape situations. If something does not seem right, get out of the situation immediately.

According to Py Bateman (1990), a common pattern exists with many acquaintance rape offenders. This pattern involves three components: (1) intrusion, (2) desensitization, and (3) isolation.

First, an *intrusion* is made into the victim's physical and/or psychological space. For example, the assailant places his hand on the victim's thigh, or his arm around her shoulder. This subtle behaviour is usually overlooked by the woman since no overt threats are made . The offender is simply 'testing out the limits.' If there is no resistance voiced by the woman for whatever reason (e.g., she is intoxicated, sleeping, unaware, or she simply does not want to make a scene), this situation could easily become out of control. Furthermore, she is likely to be *desensitized* as she tolerates her date's inappropriate behaviour. Sometimes behaviour that the victim would normally view as threatening is tolerated because a certain group of peers may reinforce its acceptance. Caution is needed when a potential aggressor addresses the possible victim in an overly familiar way. People that speak or act as if they know a person better than they actually do, indicate a warning sign of potential danger. Also, it is wise to be wary of a person who may be sitting or standing too close and seems to be enjoying the other person's discomfort. Typically, the aggressor attempts to *isolate* the victim in an area where the assault can take place. If the aggressor attempts to touch his date where she does not wish to be touched, she may push his hand away and clearly tell him 'no.' If he does not respond to subtle or gentle messages, he is no longer respecting his date. Hitting or kicking the aggressor while screaming 'no' would be an acceptable response.

The Issue of Consent

If your date touches you in a sexual way, and he does not have your consent to do so, it is considered sexual assault.

Ways to End a Date Quickly

If you believe that you are in a dangerous situation, you should do whatever it takes to get out of the situation without getting hurt. There should be no concern for the aggressor. However, should a situation develop whereby you feel uncomfortable with a date's comments and feel that things could escalate, here are some helpful ideas which may create escape opportunities.

An Emergency Phone Call. Make a phone call, or pretend to make a phone call, return to your date and inform him that something has come up and that you have to go. This could be any of a number of excuses such as an accident at home or an emergency at work.

A Trip to the Bathroom. Make a trip to the bathroom. Try to take the opportunity to call a friend or family member and invite her or him to where you are. Once that person arrives you can act surprised to see each other and invite her or him to join you.

Running into a Friend. If you do not feel comfortable with your date being alone with you in your residence, you may choose to invite a neighbour or friend over. Once again, you may choose to act surprised when the extra company suddenly appears.

Awareness Strategies to Reduce Date Rape Drug Abuse

Substances such as GHB and Rohypnol have been linked to many sexual assaults especially among young people in high schools and colleges. These sedative drugs are often being misused in party situations. About twenty minutes after an individual ingests the substance they experience disinhibition and confusion. The effects of the drug may last for hours. When the victim regains consciousness, she is likely to have no recollection of the attack. Some of the sedative drugs that are being misused can be created from home made recipes.

- Always try to watch your drink. Do not leave it out of your sight. If you do, get another one.
- At a bar or club only accept drinks from the server or a bartender.

- At parties do not accept open container drinks or drinks from punch bowls.
- Be alert to the behaviour of friends. Try to watch out for each other. Anyone who appears to be really drunk after only drinking a small portion of alcohol may have been drugged.
- If you feel dizzy, confused, or have any other unexplained symptoms after consuming a drink, get to a safe place immediately by calling a friend, the police, or 911.
- Use the buddy system. This involves making plans with friends to leave together and watch over each other at parties.
- Limit the amount of alcohol that you drink. If you are going to a party and anticipate that you will be drinking, try to eat a solid meal before the event.

Sexual Assault

I Never Called It Rape (1988) by Robin Warshaw was perhaps the largest study on sexual assault among college women. Over 6,100 students from thirty-two college campuses were interviewed. Warshaw's findings revealed that 1 in every four women surveyed were victims of sexual assault. Most victims knew their attackers (84 per cent) and 57 per cent of these rapes happened on dates. Sexual assault is the fastest growing crime in Canada and the United States.

Myths Surrounding Sexual Assault

Sexual Assault Is a Crime of Passion and Lust. Sexual assault is a crime of violence and power.

Assailants seek to control and dominate their victims.*

You Cannot Be Assaulted against Your Will. Assailants overpower their victim with the threat of violence or with actual violence. In acquaintance rapes, the aggressor often uses the victim's trust to isolate the victim.*

A Person Who Has Really Been Assaulted Will Be Hysterical. Rape survivors react differently to their experience. Emotional responses to an attack may include hysteria, calm, guilt, anger, apathy, or shock.*

Sexual Assault Is an Impulsive Act. Seventy-five per cent of all assaults are planned in advance. When three or more assailants are involved this figure rises to 90 per cent. If two assailants are involved the proportion is 83 per cent. With one assailant 58 per cent of assaults are planned.*

Assailants Are Usually Crazed Psychopaths Who Do Not Know Their Victims. As many as 80 per cent of all assaults involve either a known acquaintance, or someone the victim has had contact with, but does not know personally. Profiles on offenders reveal that they are 'normal' men who sexually assault women in order to assert power and control over them (Lenskyj, 1992).

*Asterisk indicates that this is information provided by the Tempe Police Department's *Sexual Assault Survival Course Handbook* (Tempe, Arizona, 1990).

Gang Rape Is Rare. In 43 per cent of all reported cases, more than one assailant was involved.*

Many Women Claim That They Have Been Sexually Assaulted Because They Want Revenge upon the Man They Accuse. The percentage of false reports concerning sexual assault is relatively consistent with false reports of other crimes at about 5 per cent.*

Women Who Dress or Act in a Flirtatious Way Are Asking to Be Raped. While this was a factor for some of the offenders interviewed, it is generally not the case. In fact, most offenders cannot even remember what their victim looked like.*

Women Secretly Want to Be Raped. Women and men may have sexual fantasies involving be overpowered during sexual relations. These are merely fantasies in which they are in control. No one wants the physical and emotional pain caused by this crime.*

Only Young Pretty Women Are Raped. Rape can happen to any woman or man of any age group or sexual orientation. Women are more likely to be victimized by male aggressors. Victims range in age from newborns to the elderly.*

It Impossible to Rape a Man. Men can be victimized by sexual assault. Most of these assaults involve a group of male assailants.*

If You Do Not Struggle or Use Physical Resistance You Have Not Been Sexually Assaulted. If you are forced to have sex without consent, you have been assaulted whether or not a struggle took place.*

Abusive Partners and Relationship Violence

Emotional Abuse. This is generally the first stage of relationship violence or domestic abuse. This type of abuse could be initiated randomly or it could be triggered by stress or anger felt by the offender. The woman may be used as a scapegoat for the stress or anger that originated from outside their relationship. The offender can make comments that result in the victim thinking that she is somehow inadequate. This usually involves name-calling. For example, the offender may call her stupid, fat, ugly, crazy, or sick. The goal of the offender is to crush the victim's sense of self-worth. He may try to make her feel bad about herself in a variety of ways. For instance, he may humiliate her in front of her friends or family. He may also resort to general verbal put-downs with regards to the way she looks or acts. There may be a tendency for the offender to be overly critical. He may criticize every little thing about the victim. Although emotional abuse is usually the first stage of violence, in the majority of cases this violence will continually progress into physical violence (Dutton, 1995). The following are some warning signs that you may be in a potentially abusive relationship:

- Do you feel that your relationship is 'happening' too fast?
- Is he overly jealous?
- Are you made to account for your whereabouts when you are not with him?
- Do you find yourself lying about your whereabouts just in order to keep him calm?
- Does he threaten you with violence?
- Does he threaten others with violence?
- Does he easily get angry?
- Does he make all the decisions in the relationship?
- Does he seem to criticize every little thing that you do?

Psychological Abuse. The offender may engage in stalking-type behaviour in order to try to *intimidate* the victim. She may become afraid of what he will actually do to her. Stalking-type behaviour may include: the offender following the victim or showing up unexpectedly at the victim's workplace or home. He may threaten to use violence or to abandon the relationship. This type of intimidation can widely range from a mean look to gestures or various actions such as breaking objects (especially personal objects that have a sentimental value to the victim), displaying weapons, or abusing pets. A survey based on women in shelters found that 72 per cent experienced psychological abuse, while 69 per cent suffered from threatening behaviour (Rogers, 1994).

Physical Abuse. This type of abuse may involve the offender pushing, hitting, slapping, shoving, kicking, or biting the victim. He may also use or display a weapon in order to scare the victim. Once violence is initially used, the offender may continually threaten the victim with further violence by making such comments as, 'Do you want it to happen again like last time?' One victim who was interviewed told about how terrified she was of her husband:

'He would cut out newspaper articles of women who were murdered by their husbands and then threaten me by saying that I better be careful.' Sixty-nine per cent of women in shelters experienced this type of abuse (ibid.).

Economic Abuse. The offender may control all aspects of the family finances. He will make the victim accountable for all that she spends. She may be forced to ask or plead for money, or be given a weekly allowance. If assets are placed in her name, she may still not have access to them or may not have the knowledge of how to draw from them. Perhaps he will persuade the victim not to work or go to school, but to stay home instead. This would place the victim in a more dependent relationship with the offender. Twenty-eight per cent of women in shelters experienced financial abuse (ibid.).

Sexual Abuse. This type of abuse may involve the offender raping or sexually assaulting the victim. In a relationship where a partner is forced to engage in sex, she may not consider her experience to be a rape. This is an illegal act under any circumstance. Twenty-two per cent of women in shelters experienced sexual abuse (ibid.).

Kelsey was only eighteen years old when she first began to date Rick. He was her first real boyfriend:

Case Study: Kelsey
Everything was so nice at the beginning. He really knew how to treat me right, telling me that I was so beautiful. He made me feel good about myself and I enjoyed to be

around him. A year went by and everything seemed fine. However, his attitude slowly started to change. He no longer treated me the same. There were fewer compliments, and he did not pay as much attention to me. He started to see me as an object, or as his property. He needed to control my every move. Rick did not want me to wear make-up, short skirts, or any type of sexy outfits. He did not allow me to have male friends. He did not like it when I would see my girlfriends either. He thought that all my friends were stupid. It would be very difficult for me to continue seeing them. My friends did not like him, and after a while I lost contact with them. He would try to isolate me from my family as well. One time he refused to let me visit with my brother-in-law because he thought that we would have sex. On another occasion he overheard my sister saying how we should plan a 'girls night out.' He overheard us, became upset, and replied that I am suppose to only go out with him. His character started to change gradually so it was hard for me to notice. However, the way he portrayed himself to others remained consistent. I can still clearly remember the first time he physically hurt me. We were having an argument at a bus stop. I got upset and turned away to walk home. Rick tightly grabbed my wrist and pulled me back as he demanded, 'Where are you going?' I became scared and asked him to leave me alone. Rick began cursing at me and shoved me away. I really felt weird the next day when I questioned him about the previous night's incident. When I told him that he hurt me, he acted indifferent about it, but was nice. He attempted to pretend that nothing out of the ordinary had occurred. This behaviour continued to develop. Over the next two years I experienced very abusive behaviour from him. He wanted me to respect him, but had no respect for me. It evolved into a one-way relationship. Thinking back he seemed to become the total opposite of how he first appeared to be. The relationship became much more violent in its later stages. He began to display his violence in front of his family. On one occasion I got into an argument with Rick. It got very heated, and Rick's mother stepped in to separate us. Rick's mother was leading me downstairs to the laundry room when he followed behind. He attempted to hit me and spit on me. He hit me in the face and I just left. Rick's mother told his father. His father told me not to worry and that when Rick gets older his abusive behaviour would end. We had more bad times than good times. He could be really nice during the good times. I was just trying to make it work as best that I could, thinking that we would be happy in the end.

Thinking back Kelsey feels stupid for being in the relationship, but is glad that she had the courage to end it on her own. She recalls: 'For a while I thought that it was my fault, that I had brought on the violent incidents because I chose to fight back. I would tell him that he had a problem with his temper, but he would deny it. He would blame me for not helping him control his behaviour.' Her abusive relationship provides a good example how controlling an abuser can be.

Common Controlling Strategies of an Abuser

The abuser usually suffers from low self-esteem and is more than likely to blame others for his inappropriate violent behaviour. He feels that he is within his right to abuse his partner, and he is not likely to view it as being wrong. He is likely to blame his partner for provoking his violent behaviour. He may use a variety of the tactics (e.g., instigating family arguments) to maintain power and control over his victim. He tends to adhere to the traditional male gender role of being the dominant person in the family household and the woman as being the submissive one. He is likely to have difficulty coping with stress and/or anger. He resorts to drinking and abusing his partner as a coping mechanism. He is likely to be obsessively jealous and has a controlling personality.

Many offenders have been neglected or abused as children. Many offenders have witnessed during their childhood their father being violent towards their mother. Social factors such as age, employment, negative media sex role stereotypes, and stress may sometimes play a role in the acting out of violent behaviour. For instance, unemployed young people who have a low tolerance for dealing with stress would appear to be more likely to commit violence in a relationship (Marvin, 1995).

Control

Controlling relationships usually develop over a period of time. The offender tries to maintain power and control over the victim. There is usually an attempt to control various or all aspects of the victim's life. For instance, the victim is probably not involved in any decisions. Perhaps she is not allowed to use the phone or go shopping freely. The offender has a general lack of trust in the victim. For instance, he may listen in on her phone calls. Also, he may make her strictly accountable for her whereabouts at all times. It is almost as if she has an obligation to 'report in' to him.

A controlling relationship may develop subtly. Perhaps at the initial stages of the relationship, the offender will make flattering remarks such as: 'Honey, when I am not with you, I go crazy because I love you so much' or 'Honey, I love you so much that it bothers me a bit when other guys notice you.' Eventually, this behaviour becomes intensely obsessive as the relationship develops. It may progress to the point where the offender is calling the victim, asking her where she was at certain times and who she was with. He may demand that she provide explanations as to why she went out alone. Irrational jealousy may become an issue as well. The offender thinks that the victim is cheating on him and constantly accuses her of being unfaithful. This may seem to be his motive for holding the victim accountable, however irrational it may be to anyone else. The offender may have a profound distrust towards the victim to the point where he locks her in the residence and deprives her of going to work or school. However, it may be more subtle as well. For instance, he may stop her from learning to drive. If she goes out to the store to buy a loaf of bread, she will only be given the approximate cost of the item and told to come straight home (she may be reminded that it should only take her twenty-five minutes). Victims often find themselves lying about their whereabouts and activities. Eventually, victims may live in constant fear of making the offender angry.

Isolation of the Victim

Again, because of the progression of the control, it is not likely that most women would detect the problem in its early stages. A common way of isolating the victim is by monopolizing the victim's free time, while subtly discouraging activities that are important to her and that involve people that are close to her. For instance, imagine that the victim wants to bring her new boyfriend over to meet her parents and plans a dinner date a week in advance. The day before the event, she reminds her boyfriend about it, yet he claims that he forgot all about it. In addition, he tells her he bought tickets to some special event and that if he cancels, he loses his money. The victim ends up rescheduling the dinner date with her parents and accompanies him to the event. On other attempts, the offender says he feels sick and cancels. Eventually, family members or close friends may become frustrated and stop the invitations. There is a constant attempt to separate the victim from her friends and family. The offender does not want to share her with others. It is likely that he will not like her friends or her family members. He will attempt to minimize the contact that the she has with the outside world. He may cause embarrassing episodes for the victim in front of her friends or family, or instigate family arguments forcing her to take his side out of loyalty, thereby discouraging future events. He may attempt to provoke guilt in the victim about things that she does with her friends, or concerning things that are important to her. Victims in such a situation may feel that the relationship that they are in is evolving too fast.

Abuser Drinks and/or Takes Drugs

Although some research suggests that abusive males have very high consumption levels of alcohol (Jacobson, 1993). The use of alcohol is a common way to suppress uncomfortable feelings. Anger is another way to block out these feelings. Men who have this profile also experience depression and anxiety fit into what is termed a 'dysphoric state' (Dutton, 1995). The abuser experiences dysphoric feelings as a function of his personality. Alcohol disinhibits the abuser's restraints on his own behaviour which is made up of anger. This process does not mean that alcohol causes the abuser to batter. The battering is a learned behaviour. Not every person who drinks ends up violently assaulting his partner. Alcoholism is a disease; domestic violence is not. It is a learned behaviour and therefore can usually be corrected through counselling. It is important to emphasize that alcoholism is *related* to domestic violence, but it is not the *cause* of the abusive behaviour (Davidson, 1994). Before the issue of domestic violence can be addressed, the alcoholism must be treated.

Establishing a Safety Plan, Planning to Leave

If you or someone you know is in an abusive relationship, planning ahead is most important. Victims should have a plan in place well before they attempt to leave their abusive partner. This plan should be revised on a monthly basis. Personal characteristics of the victim should be considered when developing a plan such as the victim's age, marital status, children, geographical area, resources available (financial, family, and social). In reality, first time victims are more likely to leave the abuser immediately after a violent episode when they fear for their life. These women are not likely to have a safety plan in place. In such a situation, a victim may call a crisis line and attempt to leave immediately after a violent episode. Perhaps the fight took place the prior evening and the victim chose to wait until the next morning when the abuser was out of the house (i.e., at work) before calling a crisis line or shelter. Safety plans are usually used by women who have previously been in an abusive relationship and recognize indicators that their current relationship is becoming abusive.

The Danger Level of the Aggressor

One of the first steps in creating this plan is to determine if the abuser is dangerous. Some of the questions that should be considered include the following:

- Is he capable of creating violent situations?
- Has he hit or threatened to strike, injure, or kill you?
- Does he have a history of violence?
- Does he have a criminal record and, if so, for what?
- Does he own weapons or is he skilled at using them (e.g., military service history)?

Keep in mind that when asking these questions of a victim, she may not be aware of the potential violence that her abuser is capable of. If a threat of violence is present, police involvement is recommended. The victim's best option in such a case would be to stay at a shelter.

List of Helping Resources

A list of resources should be maintained: family members, friends, and co-workers that she can trust in case of emergency, or simply for assistance through this transition. A second list should be comprised of social service contacts that have been established through past experiences. This list may include police officers, social workers, women's support staff, or other social services personnel. Make it a point to talk to someone about your situation. Do not feel ashamed to discuss this issue with friends or neighbours. Contact your local women's centre or police department for more information on helping resources in your community.

Safety during a Violent Episode

Avoid Certain Areas of a Home. Certain areas of the home are more dangerous than others during an argument. If a violent episode seems unavoidable, try to have it in a room that has access to an outside exit. Kitchens, bathrooms, or garages can be particularly dangerous places since there are many tools that can be used as weapons in these rooms.

Escaping from the Home. Think about all the possible escape routes. This should include all doors leading outside, all first floor windows, basement exits, elevators, and stairwells. It would be wise to rehearse the escape routes on a regular basis. Have a bag packed for an overnight stay and keep it at a nearby friend's or neighbour's residence in case you feel a need to leave quickly.

A Place to Go. Choose a friend or relative who will offer unconditional support. Preferably one that is not known to your partner. In many cases, the victim may not have a great deal of family support since the abuser may have alienated her from these resources. Also, a victim may not feel comfortable sharing such intimate details with family members. Many victims feel shame and embarrassment at their situation and may choose to conceal it. Victims should be encouraged to access free counselling services at local community centres or women's centres. This option can not be overstated. Counsellors can offer a great deal of guidance and support without the other complicated issues that disclosure to a family member may create. Counsellors are trained professionals who can refer clients to other resources that may be available. Victims should be cautious of religious organizations that offer counselling services. A male clergy member in most cases may not be able to meet the needs of a victim of domestic violence as well as a trained female counsellor. A motel or a women's shelter could serve as alternatives. It is important to plan this in advance, even if you do not think you will ever need to leave. Many victims do not have financial independence to initially establish their independence on their own. Others may seek a safe environment. A shelter can be a victim's best short-term alternative. If you do choose to stay at a hotel, remember to pay cash, since credit card use leaves a paper trail that will allow your abuser to find your whereabouts rather quickly. It is generally a good idea to check in under a different name.

Using Your Instincts. In a very dangerous situation you may decide that your best option is to give your abuser whatever he wants to calm him down. Using physical resistance is a personal decision that should be considered only if escaping the situation is no longer an option.

Signalling for Help. Identify one or more neighbours who you can rely on. Tell them about the situation and ask them if they can call the police if they witness any disturbance coming from your residence. Personally addressing neighbours in this way makes it harder for them to ignore the situation when it occurs.

You can also make up a predetermined code that is known to your children, family, friends, and neighbours. When they phone you or when you call them, you can use the familiar code to warn them that you are in need of assistance. For instance, a simple statement such as, 'Did you hear from Betty today?' can be the code. When people call or if you call them and state this code, they will ask you if you need help. If you indicate 'yes,' they will immediately report to the police that you are in danger. This can be an effective way to call for assistance without letting your aggressor know. Teach your children to use this same code system. A variation of this code system can also be used if a neighbour or a relative rings at your door. A similar system can be developed by flashing on and off your exterior porch light.

Helping a Friend Who Is in an Abusive Relationship

If someone who you know is a victim of domestic violence, let her know that you will be there for her. Let her know that you are willing to help her. Do not judge her, victims need support rather than scepticism:

- Never underestimate the aggressor and the potential violence that he is capable of.
- Do not put yourself between the victim and the abuser in any way. This would create a very dangerous situation for you. If you meet with the victim, try to choose a place other than the victim's home.
- Tell a victim that she is not responsible for the abuser's behaviour. Make her aware of the resources that exist in the community which may be helpful to her.
- If you witness a violent episode or overhear neighbours fighting, always contact the police. You may choose to ask that your identity not be revealed.
- Do not offer your home as a shelter to the victim without considering the fact that the abuser may continue his violent outbursts on your property or in your home. Perhaps you will also become a target of his aggression.

Cycle of Violence

In many cases a 'cycle of violence' may be established, in which the abuser experiences three stages. In the 'tension-building' stage his anger mounts to a point where he acts out abusively in the 'acute battering' stage. In the aftermath of the abusive episode the abuser may experience a 'honeymoon' stage, in which he feels remorse for his behaviour. In this stage he may apologize and promise that such abusive behaviour will never happen again. He may seem to be making positive changes toward being a better spouse or father. Despite the abuser's promise, this cycle is likely to repeat itself, and the frequency and intensity of the abusive episodes is likely to increase.

Stalking

Many stalking situations develop from domestic violence cases when the victim leaves the aggressor. Stalking is an attempt by the abuser to regain a controlling relationship with the victim. It generally involves the wilful harassment of the victim. Initially, the aggressor is obsessed with the target. The stalker may choose to court the victim by sending her notes, flowers, or making repeat phone calls. It is likely that a stalker's actions will escalate into more violent themes of harassment such as death threats to the victim and her family, vandalism, and so on.

- Report a stalking situation to the police. Contact the authorities each time a threat or sighting is made.
- Keep your own record of all incidents, dates, times, and the names of the police officers who handled the complaint. Keep a copy of all threatening letters for your own file. Make sure to keep this file in a very safe location, perhaps in a friend's home. Try to make certain that the stalker is not aware of this file.
- Do not confront the stalker, especially avoid one-on-one situations.
- Do not attempt dialogue with the stalker; he will not listen to reason.
- Tell everyone about the stalker including neighbours, co-workers, friends, and family. If possible distribute a photo of him as well. Instruct people not to give out any personal information about you or your routine.
- If the stalker does not know your address, get a post office box. Use the post office box as your address whenever possible.
- If the stalker is making harassing phone calls, do not change your number. Open a new line and keep the old line as your stalker line. This will allow your answering machine to record all of his harassing phone messages for the police.
- Consider obtaining a restraining order against the stalker. This would essentially be a court order that the stalker stay a certain distance away from you. A violation of this order would be grounds for the police to arrest the stalker. However, many stalkers are talented at intimidating their victims within the parameters of the restraining order.

Section 2: Resistance Alternatives

Offenders are usually motivated by a need to control the victim. This control can range from verbal coercion to physical violence. A victim's natural response to an assault is usually one of fear and helplessness. This response helps the offender gain control over his victim. This is an understandable reaction under the circumstances. The victim should never be condemned for having experienced this reaction. It is not the victim's fault.

The offender depends on this type of reaction and uses it to gain further control over his victim. He is not looking for a challenge or for a fight. He usually searches for the most vulnerable target that is accessible in a certain area. Reacting to an attack for most of us is a foreign experience. Our schools do not provide girls with the resources or the opportunities to effectively respond in a such a situation. Conventional female socialization in our society does not encourage women to be as aggressive or competitive as males. Therefore, a great deal of coaching and practice is required in developing the assertion and resistance techniques presented in this book so that they become second nature.

In a crisis situation a victim should try not to allow feelings of helplessness to keep her from making important decisions on how to respond. The outcome of such a situation depends on your ability to stay calm and think clearly while choosing your options. You must evaluate your chances of escaping without undue risk of physical harm. This decision must be made considering your own individual strengths and weaknesses, as well as the perceived abilities of the aggressor and the actual environment of the assault. For instance, if you feel that your verbal abilities outweigh your physical capabilities, you may choose some of the verbal strategies listed below. Resistance alternatives include any basic action on the part of the victim which results in delaying or deterring the offender. Every victim and every assailant is different. There is no one 'right' way to react to an assault. Evaluate the situation and consider any opportunities to escape. Use whatever techniques you feel are necessary and which you feel comfortable using. If something does not work, try something else. Women who have found themselves in these situations have often had to resort to many different strategies before finding one that was effective. Everyone has different strengths and weaknesses. Identifying what these are for you, before an attack, can be helpful in a crisis situation.

A landmark study on rape prevention entitled *Stopping Rape: Successful Survival Strategies*, by Pauline Bart and Patricia O'Brien (1985), revealed that certain factors were associated with victims who avoided the rape in contrast with those who did not. Women in the study who were *successful* in avoiding rape were associated with the following factors:

In childhood:
- They were likely to lack parental intervention in physical fights between siblings and friends.
- They were given parental advice to fight back.
- They were more likely to play a contact sport like football.
- They were more likely to have untraditional feminine goals.
- Their role models tended to be people who they knew.
- They were the eldest sibling.
- Their mothers had at least a college education.

In adulthood:
- They had a knowledge of first aid and self-defence.
- Many worked in high-stress jobs.
- They regularly played sports.

- They were somewhat larger than average frame (over 5'7" in height).

Women that were *not successful* in avoiding rape were associated with the following factors:

In childhood:
- Their parents commonly intervened in fights with other children.
- Their parents were less likely to give advice on how to deal with an aggressive person.
- They were likely to hold traditional or conservative expectations and goals involving marriage and family and less likely to mention career aspirations.

In adulthood:
- Their role models tended to be public figures.
- They were likely smaller than average frames (under 115 lbs in weight).
- Their fathers were likely to have high school education or less.

These findings are interesting in the process of understanding the factors associated in rape avoidance. The victim's size is initially the most apparent factor. Smaller women are perhaps more likely to be targeted by attacks by strangers since they will be perceived to be more vulnerable than larger women. This research indicates that women who challenge traditional gender roles were generally more likely to be associated with rape avoidance.

VERBAL AND OTHER NON-PHYSICAL RESISTANCE STRATEGIES

Passive Resistance

Women who passively resist an assailant are still victims of sexual assault. Passive resistance is characterized by the victim not consenting or following the orders of the assailant. Research suggests that this method of resistance is not effective in avoiding an assault (Bart and O'Brien, 1985; Ullman and Knight, 1992). Crying, begging, or pleading were also associated with being ineffective in deterring the rapist. However, choosing not to resist the attack in certain situations may be your safest option. Passively resisting the aggression does not mean that you consent. It simply means that you do what you think is necessary to survive the attack. Depending on the situation, your best option may be to passively resist. If you think you are going to be hurt, or if you are afraid to fight back, then do not. The assault is still a crime.

Assertion Strategies

An assailant may attempt to determine whether or not you are easily approachable. He may attempt to gauge your vulnerability to see if you are someone who is afraid or intimidated. At this point, being assertive with the aggressor may deter an assault even before it actually begins. If you can show the aggressor that you are angry in a firm and calm manner, he is likely to choose another target. Remember to stay calm and breathe. You will need to communicate clearly and confidently with the aggressor. Even if you are terrified, putting up a tough facade may deter him. Never be afraid to act on your instincts. If a situation makes you feel uncomfortable, let the aggressor know. This should be a basic rule, whether the aggressor is an acquaintance or a stranger. You should not be concerned about hurting his feelings, creating an embarrassing situation, or what he may think of you afterward. It is essential that you act on your instincts as early as possible. Never deny or minimize the situation. It is always better to be safe. One of your most powerful resources is your voice. If your instincts suggest danger, loudly yell out, *'No. Stop. Leave me alone ...'* Repeat your commands over and over. Do not enter into a conversation with the aggressor. Remain calm, try to support your verbal directive with a strong firm ready stance. This will be discussed at a later point in this section.

Manipulation and Negotiation

Verbal resistance can involve the use of manipulation in a number of ways. It may involve reasoning with the aggressor or distracting him from his objective. Many offenders see their victims as objects rather than as actual people. One common alternative is to attempt to appear human to the offender. For example, telling the offender that he looks like a family member.

Faking compliance at the initial stages of the attack may reduce the level of violence displayed by the offender. It is more likely that he will cooperate with you once you establish that you are complying (or pretending to comply) to his demands. For example, manipulating the offender to relinquish a weapon by telling him that he does not need to have a knife to your throat may create a new situation where he relinquishes the weapon. Telling him that you will not 'enjoy' the experience with the knife present, or that the knife is scaring you will hopefully 'con' him into putting the knife down. You may be able to have the opportunity to kick the weapon away from the area of the altercation without the assailant ever noticing. Suddenly you may have managed to disarm the assailant and now may choose to physically resist or continue with deception. If this incident is occurring in your home perhaps you may suggest, after reassuring him that you will not resist, that you go to the bathroom to freshen up. Perhaps there is a way to escape from the situation, or at least stall for time. You may choose to lock the bathroom door and crawl out the window or scream for help. A bathroom can be easily converted into a safe room for extra security (see Chapter 1). Potential victims have also verbally persuaded their aggressors to another locale by 'conning' them into believing that the secondary location is more private, and that the victim is actually looking forward to the experience. One such case involved a west coast university student who met her aggressor at a campus fraternity house party. He offered to drive her home at the end of the evening. Her friends had left early so she reluctantly accepted. On the way to her residence he decided to park on a secluded street. He started

kissing her. She protested but he would not stop. Realizing that the situation was out of control, she conned him by telling him that she would rather go to a motel room. The young man drove to a motel just off the highway. The girl suggested that she go in and register them in a room. The male happily went along – shortly afterward the young man left the hotel with four local Sheriff Deputies.

An interesting case in which verbal manipulation was effectively used concerned a woman who was sexually assaulted in her California home during a weekday afternoon. The woman attempted to reason with the aggressor as well as physically resist, but was overpowered. After the rape, the victim told the assailant that he was such a fine lover, and that she would like to see him again. She made a date with him the following evening. When he showed up at the women's door, the rapist was greeted and detained by San Jose police detectives (McNamara, 1984).

Other successful alternatives involve creating a doubt that someone will be home at any minute, or that you are not alone in your home (e.g., that your brother is upstairs). Anything to create a doubt for the rapist may confuse him. Crime prevention information sometimes recommends acting crazy, fainting, as well as vomiting or urinating on the assailant. These questionable alternatives are options that you may wish to consider; however, do so with caution. It has been stated that rape is essentially a power-based crime. The offender is not necessarily physically attracted to the victim. Some studies suggest that offenders usually cannot even remember what their victims looked like. If the rapist's motivation for the attack is to dominate or humiliate the victim, urinating or vomiting would not be much of a deterrent and could very well be interpreted by the offender as helping him achieve his goal. Perhaps urinating or vomiting in a date rape situation would have a much more deterring result.

PHYSICAL RESISTANCE

Many people feel that physically resisting a rapist is not a good option. They think that perhaps it will lead to further injury of the victim, or that the rapist will enjoy the struggle. This issue has created a great deal of confusion for crime prevention professionals who give out advice on the topic. According to the Federal Bureau of Investigation (FBI), no across-the-board answer can be given. (Harpold, 1996). FBI officials argue that before advice can be given to an individual concerning whether or not she should fight back, there are three factors that need to be considered. These factors are: the location of the incident, the personality of the victim, and the type (and motivation) of the particular rapist. The FBI maintains that no single method can prove to be effective in all sexual assault situations (Hazelwood and Harpold, 1986). For instance, a woman who successfully uses physical resistance to deter one type of rapist may lose her life by using the same resistance strategy with another type (Harpold, 1996). This research seems to be based largely on the work of the FBI's Behavioral Science Unit and contributions made from Dr Ann Wolbert

Burgess and Dr Nicolas Groth, among others. The FBI research touches upon some important issues. Most important, women need to assess their own strengths and weaknesses and develop an individual strategy that would work best for them, and a greater emphasis needs to be placed on preventing confrontational situations.

The confusion arises when we look closer at the issue. According to the FBI's own research, the largest majority of stranger rapists in our society are the 'power reassurance rapists' who are the most common and the least violent type of offender. The more violent the stranger rapist type, the less frequent he is in society (ibid.). Studies suggest that less than 10 per cent of actual rapes are reported to the police. Acquaintance rape, which accounts for about 80 per cent of all actual rapes, is generally less physically violent than stranger rape (Koss, et al., 1988). It is important to note that, although no one can provide advice with absolute certainty, physical resistance by trained women who feel comfortable using the techniques they have learned is more likely to deter an aggressor, especially when these efforts are coupled with yelling (Kleck and Sayles, 1990; Bart and O'Brien, 1985). Crying, begging, or pleading with the assailant actually increases the victim's chances of injury (ibid.). Zoucha-Jensen and Coyne (1993) found that women who use physical resistance most often avoid rape, with no greater risk of injury. Ullman and Knight (1995; 1992) support this point, and they did not find that the effectiveness of resistance strategies is related to rapist type. Also, they found that it is the level of violence that is committed by the offender that predicts how the victim is likely to respond. For instance, a victim is more likely to resist with force if she is attacked with force. Also, it is the level of force used by the offender that predicts injury to the victim (Ullman and Knight, 1992). If you feel that physical resistance is your best option, remember that you will have to hurt the aggressor seriously enough to create the time and opportunity that you need to escape.

When to Use Physical Resistance
An important distinction has to be made concerning when physical resistance should be used. In order to make this distinction, we must understand the difference between when an offender wants to take your money and/or your possessions, and when he wants to violate your body. If you are in a robbery situation you should comply. It is simply not worth the risk to use physical resistance strategies in situations to protect material possessions that can be replaced rather easily. Following the prevention advice in Chapter 1 will greatly reduce your risk of being a target.

Physical resistance should only be used when you have reasonable grounds to believe that you are about to be injured. If you believe that by resisting you have a good chance to avoid sexual assault and other grave injuries, you may choose to fight back. All other means of intervention should be considered. Is there a way to escape? Can you draw the attention of others to your situation? What are your own strengths and weaknesses? If you choose to

use physical defence strategies, you must do so with all the speed, force, and power that you can deliver. You cannot enter into the confrontation with hesitation. You have the right to defend yourself using reasonable force to deter the aggressor. You do not have the right to use physical resistance to punish your assailant after he is no longer a threat. Remember that prevention strategies are the most effective way to reduce the chances of an attack.

In his book entitled *Unleash the Lioness*, Robin Houseman (1993) best describes the issue of self-defence and the implications it has upon the law. He argues that in any self-defence situation, the victim must make every reasonable effort to avoid the confrontation and to demonstrate that she does not want to engage in an altercation. Houseman points out that if you are attacked without any warning (e.g., attacked from behind), there is no longer reason to make this clear. When using self-defence, it is within the law to use as much force as necessary to protect yourself, if it is reasonable to believe that your life is in danger. Since you do not know at what point the attack will end, it may be reasonable to assume the worst. In the aftermath, you must be able to demonstrate why you thought (at the time) that it was necessary. You are not required to justify why you chose one course of action over another, since you just instinctively reacted to the situation in order to save your life. It is important to mention that what you believe is taking place at the time is as valid as what actually happens.

Self-defence situations need to involve a real or actual threat to your safety. Houseman goes on to mention that defending yourself against a verbal threat that has been made is not good enough. However, if you believe that the same individual is about to strike you after making the verbal threat, you are justified. Factors may come up to test whether your belief was valid. For example, how close was the offender to you? Was the offender a child, man, another female, or an elderly person? Were you being threatened with violence and with no possible avenue of escape? Under these circumstances, if you felt that an assault was about to occur, it was justifiable for you to strike first. Using self-defence to punish your aggressor after he is no longer a threat is not legally justified. You must be certain that you are actually being assaulted or threatened in a way which causes you to fear for your safety. There must be an effort (whenever possible) on your part to avoid the altercation.

KEY CONCEPTS IN SELF-DEFENCE

Before focusing on the actual resistance strategies there are some important concepts that need to be discussed. They are either directly or indirectly related to a successful self-defence situation.

Awareness

Most victims who have been interviewed admit that they had not thought about what to do in such a situation, prior to the incident. The majority of people in society think that violence is something that happens in 'bad' or 'poor' neighbourhoods. Most of us still do not realize that anyone can be the victim of a personal violent crime. My mother was wrong when she told me that everything will be fine as long as I do not look for trouble. Unfortunately, trouble can sometimes find you.

Because of these realities you must recognize that anyone at any time or place can be a victim. The way in which preventing crime begins is by recognizing that you are to some degree at risk of being a victim. Although the prevention strategies mentioned in Chapter 1 will greatly reduce the risk, it is not enough. This chapter provides a detailed account of what you can do to stop an attack. It is important that special attention be focused on understanding the context in which offenders operate. If you are well acquainted with Chapter 1, it will be easier for you to recognize a potential offender.

Like any other emergency training procedure, there must be an emphasis placed upon repetition of the techniques demonstrated in this chapter. It is only through repetition that the physical movements will become less mechanical and more natural. The single most important element is to have a plan, and to think ahead. Think about your lifestyle. Identify the elements in your daily routine that you feel pose a threat to your personal safety. Think about how you could change those elements by adopting the advice given in this book. Think about certain situations were you may be harassed or attacked. Think about how you would respond. What would you say or do? Think about the places that you might be attacked in. Try to plan out escape routes, similar to a fire drill. Think about what type of resistance you feel comfortable using. Think about the precise defence that you would offer. If you are able to go through these issues in your mind, you will have mentally prepared yourself to some extent. You will be much less likely to freeze in such a situation.

Distance and Control

Most victims feel a loss of control at the beginning of an assault. For some this is from the initial point when they feel that they are being followed. Others may lose this sense of control when the offender grabs their arm. It is essential that you try to stay in control of the situation. Distance is a key element since the offender needs to get close to commit the assault. Your ability to keep a safe buffer between you and the offender may be your best way of maintaining control in such a situation. Ideally, this distance should be about three to five feet away. However, it may be much larger. Use your voice, body, or any other resources to stay in control.

Dress

According to the research, the majority of stranger rapists are not attracted to the way women dress. To repeat, most offenders cannot recall what their victims looked like. In our interviews we found offenders who matched that profile and some who actually were attracted to dress. One of the subjects was a serial rapist who was attracted to young adolescent girls. He expressed his desire to rape young girls whose breasts were just starting to develop. He would select his victims by looking for girls in his neighbourhood who during the warm summer months were wearing tight tops that revealed a bust line.

Women have a right to dress however they please. Nevertheless, the way a woman is dressed can affect her ability to resist an assault. Wearing high heeled shoes during a confrontation will limit your movement and make it more difficult to escape if you choose to run away. Tight skirts are likely to restrict movement and limit your kicking defence. It would be wiser to wear flat shoes and baggy clothes. Baggy clothes do not restrict your movement and will also conceal your female silhouette.

Purses are to be avoided. If you need to carry a purse, make sure that you keep your wallet and other valuables in a coat pocket. Any other bags or parcels that you are carrying are to be avoided as well. If you are overloaded with bags, you are more likely to be targeted.

Hit First

When most people think about self-defence they think about fighting back. Real self-defence can never be about fighting back. The term 'fighting back' presupposes that you are to wait until someone hits you first before striking out. This is a bad idea since your offender is likely to be larger, meaner, and stronger than you. In most cases, victims do not get a second chance to 'fight back.' Waiting for him to strike you would most likely result in you losing control of the situation. You do not have to be struck first to be justified in using self-defence. McIntyre (1980) found that victims who had a quick reaction to the assailant were likely to deter the rape.

A Certain State of Mind

In the Bart and O'Brien study, it was found that women who work in high-stress jobs are better able to cope with the stress of being attacked. The study also found that women who plan and prepare for a crisis before it occurs (e.g., by taking a self-defence class or first aid course) are better able to respond. A woman's perception and attitude can make a great difference in her reaction to an attack. In the same study, women who avoided rape were primarily afraid of being raped, whereas women who were raped were primarily afraid of being killed or badly injured.

A positive attitude may help keep you safe. Most of the time you are probably a friendly, polite, and kind person. You probably want to instil this behaviour into your offspring as well. Being kind and friendly to people is an admirable trait. However, there is nothing wrong with being selfish or unfriendly in certain situations to avoid an altercation. When you are alone in a secluded area, on a date with an aggressive partner, or in any other situation where you do not feel comfortable, think about 'yourself' first. Put your own interests of personal safety at the forefront of the situation, and do not second-guess yourself. Always listen to your instincts. Many women have been victimized by friends, lovers, and strangers because they did not want to overreact or cause an embarrassing scene.

When you are about to enter into confrontation, there are things that you need to know. Nothing can be such a radical departure from normal everyday life than to be involved in a physical confrontation with a larger and stronger offender. First, there are no rules. Anything that you can do to get the advantage when fighting in self-defence is acceptable. If the offender is stronger, you may choose to tell him that you will not fight back and wait for a better opportunity to resist, catching him off guard.

Using physical resistance should *surprise* your offender. Never threaten an aggressor with your skill. You do not want him to know that you have taken self-defence classes or read this book. You want him to realize it by himself as you perform the techniques on him. When practising the resistance movements, keep in mind the surprise theme. Although most of the techniques are simple and effective, they are to be implemented in a surprise fashion. For example, if you practise the same technique over and over on a larger male partner, it will lose its surprise effect, and he will eventually be able to put up effective counter-resistance to the technique. This is normal when practising with a partner. You will still have this surprise element against an offender, or anyone else who does not know what you are about to implement. To test this out, simply change partners. During the confrontation, you should not be concerned about hurting your offender or being arrested. Your main goal at this point should focus on self-protection (i.e., doing whatever it takes to either escape the situation, protect yourself, or simply survive the experience).

Escape

Escape is the most important factor. If there is a way out of a dangerous situation, take it. Even in a physical confrontation where you are physically resist-ing, if there is an opportunity to safely get away at some point in the struggle, it is best to do so. When escaping a hostile situation be careful not to turn your back on the offender if he still poses a threat. Your goal in using resistance is to use as much force as necessary to protect yourself from imminent threat of injury. Self-defence should be considered as one of several tools that can be used to get you out of the dangerous situation. It is not to be intended as a tool to punish your offender.

Physical Conditioning

The physical conditioning of a fighter is sometimes more important than fighting skill. Many amateur and professional fighters have lost to a less skilled opponent who is in better shape. Conditioning can be an important factor. If you are physically active you will be better able to apply these techniques properly in a real situation. Aerobic endurance and strength training activities are good options. Jog-ging, cycling, and aerobic dance classes are good choices to consider for keeping in shape. As men-tioned, women who have played contact sports and who currently play sports are associated with rape avoidance (Bart and O'Brien, 1985). When people freeze or get extremely nervous there is a tendency to not breathe properly. Be conscious of this. Breathe in and out; do not hold your breath. When striking a target you should be exhaling. Yelling out as you strike will help you develop a comfortable pattern. Yelling 'kia' when you strike out will give you more power as well as ensure that you are breathing prop-

erly (exhaling as you strike). You may also succeed in intimidating your opponent while yelling 'kia.'

THE BASICS

How to Stand

There are two basic ways to stand. The first is re-ferred to as the 'ready stance.' This involves stand-ing with your front foot pointed towards the offender. Your feet should be shoulder width apart with knees slightly bent. Body weight should be evenly distributed between your front and rear legs. Your torso should be slightly angled. This acts as a natural body shield and reduces your body target substantially. Rear foot position should be at a 45 degree angle with toes pointing outwards. Hands should be placed in an open position with palms facing the offender (below chest level), arms bent at the elbows. This position is also referred to as the 'assertive stance' or the 'ready stance.' This would be the position that you would assume if you felt uncomfortable (Figure 2.1).

If the situation persists or becomes more hostile, you would move into the 'fighting stance.' This is basically the same position as the 'ready stance.' The only difference is that you turn your palms inward and bring them closer in and upward to protect your face (Figure 2.2).

Where to Look

Your eyes should be focused on the neck area of the offender, keeping his entire body in your peripheral vision. Some experts suggest that you should look

Figure 2.1. Assertive stance

Figure 2.2. Fighting stance

him straight in the eye. Although this can be empowering and assertive to look into the eyes of the aggressor, you can transmit a similar message by looking at the throat area. Looking the aggressor directly in his eyes may distract you. It also may scare you. Avoid looking down, turning away, or turning your back on the aggressor. Be especially careful not to look at the area of his body that you intend to strike. This is likely to 'telegraph' your movements to your opponent.

Vital Body Targets

Primary areas to strike are those that cause the most pain and require the least amount of force. Typically they include the groin, or more specifically, the testicles. Males are well aware that this is a vulnerable target on their body and instinctively protect this region of their anatomy. In most cases, you will not have an opportunity to strike this target initially. It is still an important target and usually provides a good option for a follow-up technique. However, the throat and eyes are also extremely easy to target. If these targets are hit properly, it can cause a great deal of pain, perhaps even death to the aggressor. These three areas are known as the primary targets. Your success on physically resisting an assailant will depend on how many of these targets you can strike and how many times you can strike them with effective blows.

Secondary targets should be used to create an opportunity to strike primary targets. They can cause pain in the aggressor, but alone will not incapacitate him. This is a way to distract the opponent or take

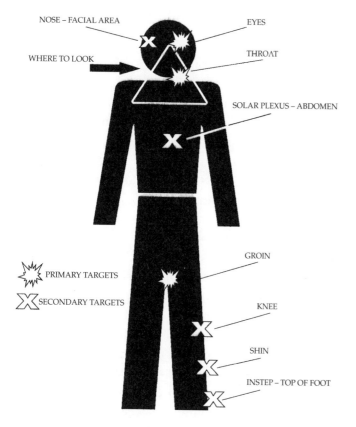

NOSE – FACIAL AREA

EYES

WHERE TO LOOK

THROAT

SOLAR PLEXUS – ABDOMEN

PRIMARY TARGETS

SECONDARY TARGETS

GROIN

KNEE

SHIN

INSTEP – TOP OF FOOT

Figure 2.3. Vital body targets

him off his guard. These areas include the instep, shin, knee joint, solar plexus, nose, hair, and facial area (Figure 2.3).

Basic Hand Strikes

Both women and men have far more strength in their legs than in their arms. Therefore, leg strikes will be much more powerful than arm strikes. However, leg strikes require much more energy to com-

plete properly. While you may feel that you do not have the strength to deliver an incapacitating blow, much will depend on hitting the proper target. For instance, an average-sized woman can strike an average-sized man directly in the chest and he may do little more than flinch. However, if that same woman directed that blow with similar force to the man's throat using the proper technique, it is likely to send him to the ground choking and coughing. It is important to remember that you must strike through your target. Similar to a runner in a race who runs past the finish line, it is imperative that you continue the striking movement through your target as well. Equally important is the fact that it is your hips that fuel the power of your all your strikes.

Open-handed techniques are preferred, rather than closed-handed techniques such as punches. Most women seem to have weaker wrists, and thus it is easy to sprain with a punch. This happens when you miscalculate your target and your wrist bends inward causing a sprain. It is also possible to injure your knuckles if you hit a hard target such as the head. If you feel comfortable using punches you may do so. It should also be noted that the palm strikes and other open-handed techniques can be even more effective than punches when executed properly. Hitting the facial area of your opponent could damage your hand. If you insist on using a closed fist, be certain that you know how to do this properly. To make a proper fist you will need to fold your fingers closed inside your palm. Your thumb goes on the outside of the rolled-up fingers, not on the inside. Your striking point should be the first two knuckles closest to your thumb.

Although there are several hand strikes available, some of the more preferred options are presented in this section.

Palm Strike

Basically this is a pushing movement similar to a violent shove. As with most of the techniques, a great deal of your power for delivering the leg and arm strikes is found in your hips. Your arm alone should not be doing the strike. Instead, power should come from your foundation (your hips), with secondary power deriving from your shoulder. If properly executed, when your right hand is striking, your left hand should be by your side. The part of your hand that makes contact with the target is the flat part of the inner, downward side of the hand. This is the section just under your end finger, but above your wrist. At this point your right hip and right shoulder should be facing the target when a right palm strike is delivered (Figures 2.4 and 2.5).

Palm Heel Strike

The palm heel when applied gently acts as a control technique. It is useful for dealing with intoxicated aggressors. To execute this technique place your palm heel on the aggressor's chin and gently but firmly push his head back. This is likely to put a safe distance between you and him (Figures 2.6 and 2.7).

If a more violent response is needed, implement the technique as an actual strike using all your power to strike upward and through the aggressor's chin

Figure 2.4. Palm strike

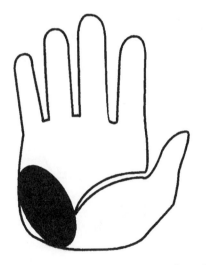
Figure 2.5. This blackened region represents the striking surface of the palm strike

Figure 2.6. Palm heel strike

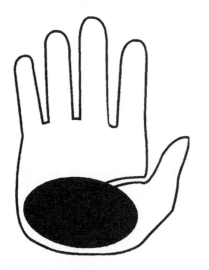

Figure 2.7. This blackened region represents the striking surface of the palm heel strike

with the heel of your palm, while keeping all fingers rigid in either an open or closed position (Figure 2.8).

Clawing Palm Heel
The clawing palm heel is a more devastating option and should only be used in extreme situations. All four fingers are open and rigid, the thumb is kept back out of the way. Claw into the opponent's eyes as you shove the heel of your palm into the aggressor's chin. For even better results consider shoving your palm heel into the bridge of the aggressor's nose while clawing his eyes. This will cause greater pain for the aggressor (Figure 2.9).

Open Hand Throat Strike
Using the open space between your thumb and your index finger as the weapon, strike your opponent's throat or Adam's apple with full force. This technique is delivered similar to all hand strikes. Power should be coming from your hips and shoulders rather than your arms. You will have to twist your upper body as you strike towards your target. A right-handed throat strike should cause your right shoulder to be pointed towards the opponent as the strike reaches its target (Figure 2.10).

Thumbing Eye Gouge
Your hands should be placed on both sides of the attacker's face. You may choose to grab onto his hair if it is long enough, or grab onto his ears. The palms of both hands should be placed on the aggressor's cheek bones. Place your thumbs into his eyes and plunge into them deeply (Figure 2.11).

Figure 2.8. Palm heel strike

Figure 2.10. Open hand throat strike

Figure 2.9. Clawing palm heel

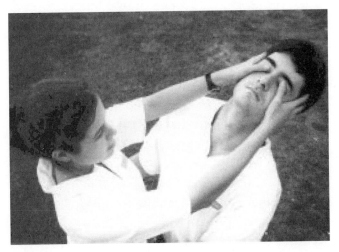

Figure 2.11. Thumbing eye gouge

In some circumstances this is an ideal strategy since it allows you many options. Theoretically, you could place your hands on both sides of the attacker's face in an attempt to push him away. It is likely that the aggressor will have no clue that you have set up the thumbing eye gouge technique. If you choose to implement the gouge you are likely to catch the assailant with great surprise. Some women may not feel comfortable carrying out such a strategy. If this is the case, be certain that if you decide to implement this technique, you do not hesitate during its execution. If performed properly you will cause serious injuries to your opponent. The aggressor may permanently lose his vision, have long-lasting sight impairments, or experience immediate and severe shock.

Groin Grab

Unique opportunities may arise if you are in close range of the assailant. In most situations a male's testicles are an extremely sensitive body part and provide you with a good target. Whether you are facing the aggressor or if he has a hold of you from the back, the groin can be targeted in close range with hardly any skill of self-defence. The major factor involved is mentally conditioning yourself to instinctively attack the target. This technique can be performed from both the front and the rear. It is a very quick movement in which you reach up and grab hold of the attacker's testicles. Grabbing the penis will not be as effective as grabbing his testicles. You need to be certain that you reach between the legs and grab the testicles. This technique is more difficult to execute if the attacker is wearing tight-fitting jeans. If this is the case, you can strike at the groin with a fist, knee, or foot. It should also be noted that in the rare case where an offender is extremely intoxicated or high on drugs he may not be vulnerable to this technique (Figure 2.12).

Figure 2.12. Groin grab

Forearm Groin Strike

In a situation where the aggressor grabs hold of you from behind and places one arm around your neck, the forearm strike is an effective technique. It involves clenching your hand into a fist, bringing your arm upwards and then sending it back into the aggressor's groin area. It is the under part of your forearm that makes contact with the groin. If executed properly your hand should be able to be seen by another person standing behind the aggressor. If the attacker is farther away, you may choose to strike the groin with your fist (Figure 2.13).

Front Upward Elbow Strike

As with all elbow strikes, this technique is best used when the aggressor is extemely close to you

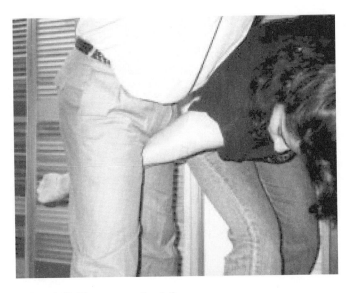

Figure 2.13. Forearm groin strike

Figure 2.14. Frontal linear elbow strike

(i.e., closer than arm's length or in kissing distance). There are four basic striking options. Front upward strikes involve moving your elbow upward under the opponent's chin or solar plexus. As you begin you should be standing directly facing the aggressor. The starting point of this strike would involve your elbow being in a lowered position (e.g., beside your rib cage). To execute this technique, simply deliver an upward strike by bringing your elbow up to the target from a lower position. You will want to twist your body so that if you are striking with your right elbow, your entire right side will twist forward towards your opponent upon impact. It is the forearm side of your elbow that should make contact with the intended target (Figure 2.14).

Rear Linear Elbow Strike

Rear upward strikes are usually used when you have your arms free and are grabbed from the side, or when an opponent puts his arm around your shoulders. Again, this type of defence is intended for close-quarter fighting. Your primary targets should include the opponent's groin, solar plexis, or facial area. For best results, the aggressor would virtually have to be right up against you side by side. Reinforce the striking arm with your other arm by making a fist with the striking arm and then placing the palm of your other hand over that fist. Bring both your arms forward (straightening them outward), away from yourself and the opponent to gain momentum. Begin bending the elbow as you throw it into your target. Deliver the strike with a powerful effort while slightly pivoting your hips. Be sure to look back to see where you are hitting. The contact point of your strike is the top part of the elbow (lower triceps area; Figure 2.15).

Front Roundhouse Elbow Strike

Frontal roundhouse strikes involve moving your elbow inward in a circular fashion across the centre of your chest making contact with the side of the opponent's head or facial area. These strikes can be thrown from either the lead or rear arm. Your body should twist at the hips while delivering the strike and your lead foot should pivot in the same way as your lead shoulder. The contact point for this strike is the lower part of the elbow (upper, outer forearm area; Figure 2.16).

Reverse Roundhouse Elbow Strike

This strike option is similar to a back hand slap. In order to launch a powerful strike, you will need to bring your arm across your body. For instance, if you intend to strike with a right reverse round-house elbow , you will need to bend your elbow at the joint. Bring your right hand across so that it touches beyond your left shoulder. Then you are in position to launch the strike. Your contact point is the top part of the elbow (lower triceps area). Your target is usually the aggressor's chin, throat, or facial area. Reverse roundhouse strikes are usually used when your opponent is facing you within kissing distance (Figure 2.17).

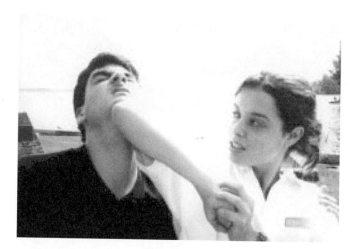

Figure 2.15. Rear linear elbow strike

Figure 2.16. Frontal roundhouse elbow strikes

Figure 2.17. Reverse roundhouse elbow strikes

Figure 2.18. Blocks

Figure 2.19. Blocks

Basic Blocks

To block an opponent's strike you will need to inter-
cept and redirect his strike. This will knock the strike
off its course and prevent it from hitting the intended target. If the attacker attempts to strike you
with a basic straight punch using his right fist, from
your fighting stance assume a left lead (left arm and
leg in front). Step back out of striking range to evade
the full force of the blow. Use your left hand to
deflect his strike by slapping away his wrist with
your palm or forearm. You should be able to redirect the strike inward and away from the intended
target (Figures 2.18 and 2.19).

Most offenders tend to strike the facial area of
their victim with their right hand. This information
helps make the typical opponent somewhat predictable. Inside blocks involve deflecting the strike
inward and away from its intended target. To practise this technique stand in your fighting position.
Have a partner push you in the centre part of your
upper chest just beneath your throat. This should be

done gently. At first, do not resist. If your partner is pushing properly it should knock you off balance, forcing you to take a step back in order not to fall. This is a worthwhile exercise for both parties since the person pushing will learn how to properly strike through the target. Equally important is the opportunity to practise how close you should be to execute a proper strike. Many students who begin this exercise launch ineffective strikes because they position themselves too far away from their target. This causes them to lunge forward in an off-balanced position as they strike. Many students are unable to strike through the target for maximum power because they are standing too far away from their opponent. A fundamental rule is that students should be striking about five inches through the intended target. This means that if you wanted to strike someone in the nose, you would make certain that you were close enough to strike about five inches beyond that point. The student practising blocking skills will learn how to deflect the strike from its intended target with as little force and effort as necessary.

Outside blocks are used to protect against hook punches, backhand strikes, and circular strikes. When you are in your fighting stance, your hands should be protecting your head area and your elbows should be tucked in protecting your rib cage (Figure 2.20).

You are ready to block a strike and execute an outside block from this position. However, if your opponent is much stronger than you it would be wiser to step back and avoid the strike than to block

Figure 2.20. Blocks

it. You may not have enough upper body strength to execute a full block.

Basic Leg Strikes

As previously mentioned, although leg strikes can provide a very powerful strike, they require more energy than hand strikes. All kicks that will be introduced are basic and easy to learn. It is not recommended that you attempt to strike at target areas on your opponent that are higher than the opponent's mid-section with a kick. Fancy spinning kicks to high targets are mostly used in tournament competition and have no place in realistic self-defence manoeuvres. It is important to develop a swift and balanced kicking style.

Front Kick

The front kick is a basic kick that is intended to be

Figure 2.21. Front kick

Figure 2.23. Front kick

Figure 2.22. Front kick

delivered to the opponent's solar plexis or mid-section region. This is the area between the opponent's mid-section just under their ribcage. From your 'fighting stance' position, lift your back leg drawing it close to your body. You will need to bend your knee close so that your thigh is brought up into your body. This is called 'chambering' your leg (Figures 2.21 and 2.22).

As you extend your leg towards the target, you should thrust your hips slightly forward to give yourself more power. Your standing leg should be slightly bent for better balance (Figure 2.23).

The part of your foot that should make contact with the target is the ball of your foot (your foot should be positioned as if you were wearing high heeled shoes, your toes should be flexed in an upward position). Kick out through your target. Always attempt to strike beyond the point that you are striking. This will ensure maximum speed and power in your strike. The target that you should be kicking at is the solar plexis of the aggressor which is located just under the ribcage. After striking the target quickly bring your leg back into the chambered position before going back into your fighting stance. This is to ensure that the opponent does not grab your kicking leg while it is extended. Always remember to return the kicking leg to this chambered position with the same speed as the actual kick. Try to remember to focus your sight at the neck area of the aggressor. Never look at the area that you intend to strike, as this will telegraph your intentions to the opponent.

Figure 2.24. Groin kick

Groin Kick

The groin kick is essentially the same kick except that your target is the opponent's groin. It is your shin, not your instep that makes contact with the groin. In order to strike the target properly, you must make certain that you kick between the opponent's legs. This means that if your kick is properly executed, your foot should be able to be seen by people standing behind the opponent (Figure 2.24).

Again, this kick is similar to the front kick. You need to chamber your back leg by drawing it close in to your body, bending it at the knee. As you launch it forward allow the opponent's legs to help guide the kick upward towards the target. Your shin makes contact with the groin, not your instep. Your toes should be curled. This makes it a much harder kick and lessens the chance that you will miss the target. As you extend and straighten your leg, slightly thrust your hips forward for extra power. Your standing leg should remain slightly bent for better balance. Again, remember to bring the kicking leg back quickly into the chambered position before going back into your fighting stance.

Side Kick

For realistic self-defence purposes there are actually two basic targets for this kick. The most practical is the knee target. Executing a side kick to an opponent's knee requires a minimal amount of balance and flexibility. The second target involves striking

Figure 2.25. Side kick

Figure 2.27. Side kick

Figure 2.26. Side kick

the opponent's mid-section, either the solar plexus, or if executed from his side, his ribcage. To execute a side kick stand with your side facing your opponent. Lift the leg closest to the opponent and chamber it by bringing it in close to your body, bent at the knee (Figures 2.25 and 2.26).

Simply kick outward directly to the knee joint. Your heel should make contact with the target for best results (Figure 2.27).

For executing a higher strike to the mid-section, the kick will require an advanced level of flexibility and balance. Essentially it is the same kick, but you will need to use your hips more as you pivot on your standing foot (your standing foot will pivot on your toes so that the heel faces towards the opponent).

Figure 2.28. Back kick

Figure 2.29. Back kick

Back Kick

The back kick is effective and appropriate to use when the attacker is behind you, perhaps holding you from behind. To execute an effective back kick, chamber your leg in front of you bringing it close in to your body. Lift your kicking leg so that the top part of your thigh is touching, or nearly touching the lower part of your mid-section (Figures 2.28 and 2.29).

As a general rule, the higher that your target is, the more forward you will have to lean. For self-defence purposes your primary targets for this kick should include the opponent's knee joint or groin area. When delivering a back kick to the groin area of the aggressor, slightly bend your upper body forward at the waist. This will make it possible to hit a higher target more easily

Heel Stomp

The heel stomp is perhaps the simplest leg strike. Although easy to implement, it will not incapacitate your aggressor and is less effective than other leg strikes to the knee joint or the groin area. It is most effective as a distraction which creates the opportunity for a more devastating follow-up strike. To execute the heel stomp lift the leg closest to your opponent up so that your thigh is parallel to the ground and then stomp down on his instep using your heel as the weapon (Figures 2.30 and 2.31).

Knee Strike

Knee strikes are often used as a follow-up technique. They can seriously injure the opponent with relatively little effort on your part. There are three

Figure 2.30. Heel stomp

Figure 2.31. Heel stomp

basic targets for an effective knee strike: the facial area, the solar plexis, and the groin. Although it has been stressed that it is not worth while to deliver fancy high kicks above the opponent's mid-section, this leg strike is the one exception. Best delivered after a groin kick, knee strike, or any other technique that would cause the opponent to become momentarily disillusioned, its result could be lethal. To execute, grab hold of the opponent's head and pull it down as you raise your knee upward though the target. You will want the opponent's facial area to make contact with the top part of your knee (Figures 2.32 and 2.33).

Fighting in Sequence

It is likely that you will need more than one strike to incapacitate your aggressor. Combinations are basic fighting sequences made up of three or four striking techniques that you can develop on your own. You can practise executing these techniques in a certain rehearsed order until they become second nature. At first you may choose a more basic option. From a fighting stance where you have your left foot forward and your left arm is your lead (hand closest to the opponent) a possible option would be: palm strike (left), palm strike (right), and groin kick (either leg).

As you practise developing your combinations you will become more familiar with the movements involved in the actual techniques. A more difficult combination would involve not only a mix of hand and leg strikes, but also a variation of high and low target options. To further confuse the opponent you will

Figure 2.32. Knee strike

Figure 2.34. Fighting in sequence

Figure 2.33. Knee strike

want to strike at one of his higher targets right after striking a lower target. Perhaps one of the easiest, yet most devastating combinations involves the thumbing eye gouge followed by the groin kick, ending with a knee strike to the head (Figures 2.34 to 2.36).

Release Defences

The basic element to remember concerning any type of hand grab whether to your wrist or your elbow is that it is only as strong as the opponent's thumb. The weakest point of his grip will be exactly were his thumb meets his fingers. You will want to apply quick pressure against this point. You should not attempt to enter into a wrestling match with the aggressor by using a pulling motion. It is not likely to work in freeing you and will only drain you of your energy. He will usually be stronger than you, and is likely to win the fight if it becomes a wres-

Figure 2.35. Fighting in sequence

Figure 2.36. Fighting in sequence

tling match. Your best defence centres on using a properly executed technique. The element of surprise will be your greatest asset. Most offenders expect their victim to put up a moderate struggle; they do not expect them to put up effective resistance. The aggressor may choose to grab your wrist, elbow, or shoulder. While it is recommended that you focus your energy on directly breaking the actual hold, you could also resort to using any of the leg or arm strikes as either a diversionary tactic or as an alternative to executing a wrist or elbow grab defence.

Two Hands Grabbing One Wrist

If the aggressor grabs a hold of one of your wrists with both his hands, you will have to respond quickly. Make a fist with the hand that has been grabbed. Reach in between both of his arms and grab hold of that fist with your free arm. Pull upward and back towards yourself bending both arms at the elbow. Be careful when practising not to strike yourself in the face as you pull your wrist back to your shoulder. Although this will break the aggressor's hold, you may have to execute a follow-up strike (Figures 2.37 to 2.39).

One Hand Grabbing One Wrist

If the attacker grabs hold of one wrist with only one of his hands, the above-mentioned technique should also work providing the thumb is placed on top of the wrist. Another option is to rotate the same forearm in a circular inward then outward motion as you pull back towards yourself (Figures 2.40 to 2.42).

Be careful, sometimes there is the rare case where

Figure 2.37. Two hands grabbing one wrist

Figure 2.39. Two hands grabbing one wrist

Figure 2.38. Two hands grabbing one wrist

Figure 2.40. One hand grabbing one wrist

the opponent will unintentionally use a reverse grip. This means that the thumb would be on the underside of your wrist. In this case you would have to apply pressure in a downward motion as you pull

back towards yourself. You will need to bend your front knee slightly as you pull downward. As long as you are able to determine where the opponent's thumb is in the grip and apply pressure to that

Figure 2.41. One hand grabbing one wrist

Figure 2.43. One hand grabbing one wrist

Figure 2.42. One hand grabbing one wrist

Figure 2.44. One hand grabbing one wrist

point, it will be difficult for the offender to maintain his grip. It should be noted that the larger your wrists are, the easier it will be to implement this technique. In this situation, the aggressor grabs your wrist and attempts to pull you away (Figure 2.43).

You can simply put pressure on his thumb by moving your wrist upward and to the outside against his thumb (Figure 2.44).

Figure 2.45. Two hands grabbing two wrists

Figure 2.47. Two hands grabbing two wrists

Figure 2.46. Two hands grabbing two wrists

Two Hands Grabbing Two Wrists

If the offender grabs hold of each of your wrists with each of his hands, you will need to reverse the grip if possible by rotating your open hands inward

and around his wrists. The objective is not to break his hold, but to launch a quick and effective counterstrike. It is not important if he maintains his hold at this point. Pull him towards you while you deliver a knee strike to his groin or a groin kick at the same time. It is essential that you do your best to pull him towards you as your knee strike is delivered. This technique, especially the pulling and knee strike, requires a quick surprising action that will catch the aggressor off guard (Figures 2.45 to 2.47).

Elbow Grab Behind Your Back

In this scenario the offender has both his hands trapping your arm behind your back. One hand is holding your elbow while the other is on your wrist. To escape this hold you must go in the direction that the offender's grip is pushing you in and spin yourself around so that you are facing him as you

Figure 2.48. Elbow grab behind back

Figure 2.50. Elbow grab behind back

Figure 2.49. Elbow grab behind back

straighten out your elbow. You have now broken free from the elbow grab, to break free from the wrist hold simply twist your wrist against his thumb (Figures 2.48 to 2.50).

Rear Elbow Grab
If the aggressor grabs hold of both your elbows from behind, the thumb position of his grip will be facing upward. To escape the hold follow the direction of his pull. Try to bring your arms upward from behind. Straighten your arms as you move them outward and around the assailant's grip (Figures 2.51 to 2.53).

Front Elbow Grab
The offender grabs your right elbow with his right

Figure 2.51. Rear elbow grab

Figure 2.53. Rear elbow grab

Figure 2.52. Rear elbow grab

Figure 2.54. Front elbow grab

Figure 2.55. Front elbow grab

Figure 2.57. Rear/side shoulder grab

Figure 2.56. Front elbow grab

Figure 2.58. Rear/side shoulder grab

Figure 2.59. Frontal shoulder grab

Figure 2.61. Frontal shoulder grab

Figure 2.60. Frontal shoulder grab

hand. This technique is very similar to the wrist release technique. To escape, you will need to raise your forearm up and over his thumb. As you straighten out your arm, you will break his grip. If the aggressor holds each of your elbows with each of his hands, use the same technique on both arms. Simply bring your forearms up and apply pressure to the thumbs by rotating the forearms over his thumbs as you straighten your arms (Figures 2.54 to 2.56).

Rear or Side Shoulder Grab – Swing Defence Arm Lock

If the aggressor grabs hold of your shoulder, straighten your arm and swing it forward right around the offender's grip. The swing action will break the offender's grip. You may be able to lock the aggressor's arm between your rib cage and upper arm if this technique is performed properly (Figures 2.57 and 2.58).

Front Shoulder Grab – Swing Defence

If the opponent grabs hold of both your shoulders and pushes you backward, swing your straightened arms using an inside circular motion sending your arms up and over the aggressor's hold. It is possible to trap his arms, if executed properly. If you manage to trap his arms between your upper body and your upper arms (just under your armpits), you can execute an effective leg strike or head butt as a follow-up (Figures 2.59 to 2.61).

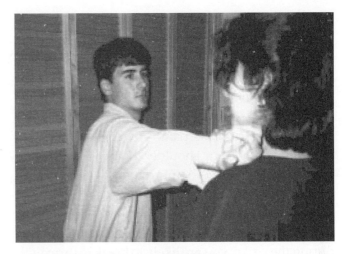

Figure 2.62. Frontal shoulder grab

Front Shoulder Grab

The simplest option in this situation requires a quick release (inside block) and a powerful groin kick. However, there are many effective alternatives that can be implemented. If the aggressor grabs hold of your left shoulder with his right hand, you may be able to execute a control hold on him. Use your right hand to turn his palm in a clockwise motion so that the back of his hand faces upward while it rests on your left shoulder. His arm will need to be fully extended for this technique to work. Use your left hand to put pressure just above his elbow (triceps area) with a constant downward force, while holding his palm with your right hand. Keep the pressure on his joint as you slightly lift his hand upward. If executed properly the opponent should be able to be escorted to the ground face first. You will need to practise gently with a partner. It may take some time to master this movement (Figures 2.62 and 2.63).

Figure 2.63. Frontal shoulder grab

A wrist lock can be added to the elbow joint lock (arm lock) by twisting the wrist inward with your right hand and maintaining a downward pressure with your left arm.

Another option involves breaking the opponent's elbow. This is executed in a similar fashion. Use your right hand to turn his palm upward and keep his hand pinned to your shoulder. Rather than putting pressure on the elbow joint, chamber your left arm by moving your hand behind your head. Next, send out a circular strike to the elbow joint with all your force. If you keep his palm pinned to your shoulder during the strike, you are likely to break his arm with your forearm (Figures 2.64 and 2.65).

Defences Against Hair Pulls

You can minimize the discomfort of the hair pull by gripping hold of the aggressor's hand and clamping it down on your head. If you have longer hair, perhaps you can grip your hair at a closer point to your head and pull it towards your scalp. It is likely that this effort will take up one or both of your hands. Therefore, you should rely upon a leg strike to deter the aggressor. A swift low side kick to the knee or groin kick might be appropriate. If you happen to miss your target, keep kicking. The fact that the offender has a hold of your hair means that one of his hands is not free. Be aware of his free hand (know where it is at all times), as it might be used to slap or hit you (Figure 2.66).

Trips and Take-Downs

Sending the aggressor to the ground may give you

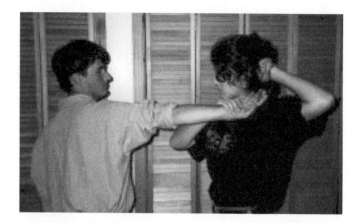

Figure 2.64. Frontal shoulder grab

Figure 2.65. Frontal shoulder grab

the edge in a confrontation. There are several simple manoeuvres that can be used to accomplish this goal. It is crucial that you use the element of surprise in all self-defence manoeuvres. This is especially true with the various trips and take-down options presented in this section. The success of any self-defence move will depend on your ability to

Figure 2.66. Hair pulls

Figure 2.67. Take downs

execute the technique swiftly and quickly. The element of surprise will aid in this process. Practising all the techniques on a frequent basis will help them develop into natural movements, making them seem less mechanical in the long term.

Front Leg Sweep

If the aggressor has a hold of your shoulder with his hand, you may be able to send him crashing to the floor if you can execute this technique with surprise. It is not likely to work if the assailant knows what you are trying to do. Therefore, when practising with a partner it should work well the first few times. It is likely that your partner will balance himself differently after the first few falls. This is fine. Remember that the element of surprise is impor-

Figure 2.68. Take downs

tant. When practising with your partner through several repetitions you are certain to lose this advantage. Do not get discouraged. You can always try it out on a new practise partner once it is perfected. It should work the first couple of times with every new partner. Another option would be to execute different manoeuvres in a random order so that he has no idea what you will execute next.

If the aggressor grabs your shoulder with his hand from the front, take your right foot and move it out and around the aggressor's right leg (Figure 2.67). Place your leg behind his and lean forward as you push through the aggressor's throat with your right hand (Figure 2.68).

Although the aggressor is likely to release his hold as he falls, there are rare situations in which the aggressor maintains the hold bringing the victim to the ground on top of him. If this occurs, make sure that you land directly on the aggressor, as this will cushion your fall and maximize his pain. Try to execute a follow-up technique. It is important that you stay on top of him. You would be at a very large disadvantage if he were to be on top of you. See the ground techniques section for more information about this situation.

Another variation of this technique is to slightly move your right hip towards the aggressor as you send your straightened right leg upward and forward, past the side of his right leg (waist high; Figure 2.69 and 2.70).

Use the momentum of your returning leg to buckle the rear knee joint of the aggressor at an outer angle. At the moment that your leg (calf) makes contact

Figure 2.69. Take downs

Figure 2.70. Take downs

Figure 2.71. Take downs

Figure 2.72. Take downs

with the outer rear of the aggressor's knee joint, you push him back by striking him in the face or throat area (or straight downward if performed violently; Figures 2.71 and 2.72).

Front Hip Trip

This technique also relies upon a swift surprise movement You will need to exercise caution as you execute this technique. As you implement the trip, you will be briefly putting yourself off balance. In this situation you must strike quickly since you are susceptible to the exact same technique if launched by the aggressor as a counter-move. Another defence against a frontal hug, this trip can be used at almost any time the aggressor is in close range (his body centre must not be more than two feet away from you). To execute this technique, simply bring your right foot outside his right leg so that your hip side is touching his hip side (Figures 2.73 and 2.74).

At this point, your right foot will almost be behind his right foot. Grab hold of his left shoulder with your right arm. This should place your right arm across his chest. Apply a twisting pressure as you push his upper body towards and over your hip (Figure 2.75).

Step to the Back of the Knee

This technique is extremely effective if the aggressor has his back or side turned towards you. Simply executing a side kick to the aggressor's knee joint from the side would most likely result in a fracture if executed properly. However, as a control technique stepping on the back of the knee will send the

Figure 2.73. Hip trip

Figure 2.75. Hip trip

Figure 2.74. Hip trip

aggressor off balance. To execute start off by delivering a side kick to the back of the upper part of the leg. Initial contact will be made with his hamstring. Your kick should forcibly slide downward, causing his knee to buckle. As the knee bends forward you will need to apply pressure to the top of the calf, pushing it into the ground (Figure 2.76).

Ground Techniques

There seems to be a great deal of controversy concerning ground fighting among self-defence instructors. Most argue that the worst place to be in a fight is on the ground, especially when the opponent is standing. Other schools have just the opposite perspective encouraging their students to purposely fall to the ground when they believe

Figure 2.76. Step to the back of the knee

that a physical confrontation is eminent. The rationale behind their advice seems to be rooted in the idea that women can avoid the injury of being thrown down by their aggressor. In any case, it is not recommended to go to the ground first. Staying away from the ground is generally a good idea. If you fall to the ground with the assailant, try to fall on him rather than under him. Do not to let him fully pin you to the ground. This can be accomplished by using your legs to kick at him from the basic ground defence fighting position. Be cautious to stay face up (resting on your back), rather than face down (chest resting on the ground) if the assailant positions himself on top off you. In a face-down position the use of your arms, legs, and hips will be severely limited.

GROUND FIGHTING DEFENCE POSITION

The general fighting position when you are on the ground involves keeping your best leg ready to strike. Lie on your hip side (buttock) opposite your strongest leg, using your forearm and elbow to support your upper body. Always face the opponent; try to keep your legs between him and you. To keep him away from you, deliver kicks to his groin area or his knees when he is standing, or to his facial area or collarbone if he is on the ground. Your heel is the contact point for this kick (Figure 2.77).

If he attempts to move around you, shift yourself so that you maintain a position where your feet are facing the aggressor. Many students make the mistake of trying to get up from the ground too soon, turning their back towards the aggressor as they attempt to stand up. Never lose sight of the assailant. Make sure that he is either disabled or far enough away (i.e., at least eight feet away from you) so that you can get up safely assume a fighting stance or escape from the situation.

Ground Defence Against a Standing Offender
This technique is more of a take-down manoeuvre. It involves trapping the aggressor's leg in a straight extended position while forcing it backwards, sending him off balance. To properly execute this take down from the ground you must slip the foot (instep or heel) of your lower leg behind the heel of the aggressor's closest foot. You would then firmly place your higher leg to the top part of the knee joint and apply a constant push, while simultaneously apply-

Figure 2.77. Ground defence fighting position

Figure 2.78. Ground defence against a standing offender

ing a pulling tension inward towards you with the heel of your other leg that is secured behind his foot (Figure 2.78).

Another version of this technique could be used to fracture the leg of the aggressor. To execute the breaking manoeuvre you would need to follow all the same points. However, rather than applying pressure with the kicking leg, chamber the kicking leg close to your body, while you still have his closest foot secured with the heel of your other foot. Follow up with a smashing blow directly on the knee cap with all your force.

Ground Defence against Front Pins

In this situation, the aggressor is holding you down and sitting across your waist while pinning your arms above your head. He uses his body weight to trap you to the ground. This is a very difficult situation to escape from, especially if you do not have a great deal of upper body strength. The aggressor expects you to resist and attempt to push him off of you. It is very important to make the element of surprise work for you in this situation. Pushing upward will do little. The aggressor is leaning forward with all his body weight. It should be noted that the aggressor is not likely to stay in this position. He will need to free his hands to remove his and your clothing. In this situation he cannot do anything further to you without changing his position. In most cases, there will be opportunities to escape during the assault. To escape from this situation you will need to bend both your legs bringing them right up close so that your thighs are against the attacker's buttocks (Figure 2.79).

Make sure to keep your heels on the ground. Your next and most difficult task is to lower your arms at least to eye level, but preferably to beneath shoulder level. This can usually be accomplished by suddenly jerking them downward without warning. You may choose a diversionary tactic such as biting the assailant's forearm to help you along. Jerking your arms downward below shoulder level may or may not break his hold. His hands could follow as you move your arms downward. As soon as they begin to come downward, simultaneously thrust your waist upward in the air lifting your buttocks off the ground. Once you are successful in throwing the aggressor off of you (Figure 2.80), immediately go into your ground defence fighting position (Figure 2.77).

The assailant should be off balance. Ideally he will be sent over you. Once your hands are free use them to push him away. Sometimes when jerking the hands downward the aggressor's grip is broken (Figures 2.81 and 2.82).

If this occurs you can trap one of his arms in your armpit between your upper arm and your ribcage by passing your arm upward and around his, pulling it into your ribcage (Figures 2.83 and 2.84).

When trapping the opponent's arm, it is important that you apply a tight controlling squeeze so that he cannot pull it away and out of your hold. If your other hand is free, place it in the aggressor's face, gouging his eyes. Use the same hip thrust and direct him with your gouging hand towards the side of the arm trap. If your other arm is pinned, you may still be able to execute this move by lifting

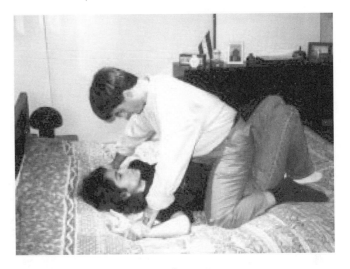

Figure 2.79. Ground defence – front pins

Figure 2.80. Ground defence – front pins

your hips towards the trapped arm side. Do not let go of the aggressor's trapped arm. Once you are successful in throwing the aggressor off of you, im-

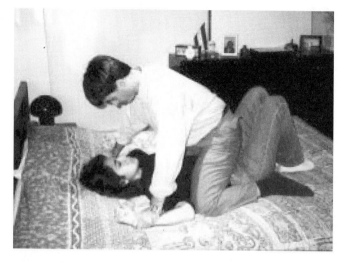

Figure 2.81. Ground defence – front pins

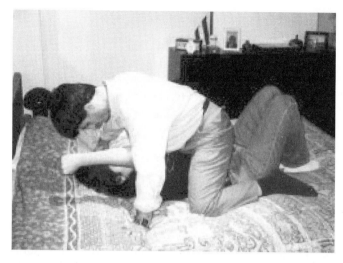

Figure 2.83. Ground defence – front pins

Figure 2.82. Ground defence – front pins

Figure 2.84. Ground defence – front pins

mediately go into your ground defence fighting position (see Figure 2.77).

Front Pin and Strangle

The frontal strangle appears to be more difficult to escape from, but it really is a lot simpler to get out of than it appears. Since both of the attacker's hands are on your throat, you must act quickly. Use your strongest arm, pass it upward through the attacker's arms and then outward towards your side in a

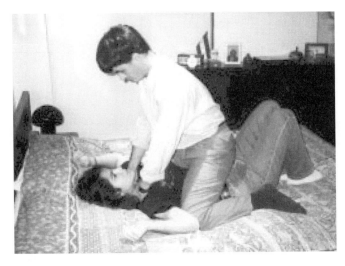

Figure 2.85. Ground defence – front pins

Figure 2.87. Ground defence – front pins

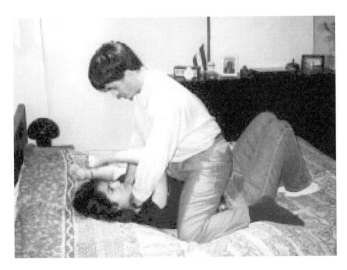

Figure 2.86. Ground defence – front pins

circular motion. Your biceps should make contact with his wrist or forearm (Figures 2.85 and 2.86).

You should be able to break his hold from your throat and trap it by your side in and against your

rib cage exactly as outlined in the previous technique (Figure 2.87).

You will need to follow the exact same lower body movements as mentioned in the previous technique. Again, remember to execute a tight hold so that the opponent does not have the opportunity to pull his arm out of your hold. Your other hand gouges the aggressor's eyes as you thrust your waist straight up off the ground and direct your attacker with your gouging hand towards and over his trapped arm. Once you are successful in throwing the aggressor off of you, immediately go into your ground defence fighting position (see Figure 2.77).

Front Pin – Aggressor Seated on Victim's Chest
In this situation, the aggressor is seated across the top of the victim's chest. As he pins her arms by her side with the inside of his knees, he is attempting to force his victim to perform oral sex (Figure 2.88).

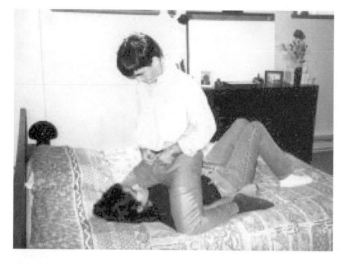

Figure 2.88. Front pin – seated

Figure 2.90. Front pin – seated

To escape from this position, you will need to bring both your legs upward and in front of the aggressor. Your buttocks should lift off the ground as you swing your legs upward. Anchor both heels onto the front side of each of the opponent's shoulders and pull him backwards to the ground. This technique requires a fair amount of flexibility. Taller students usually have an easier time implementing this strategy. Once you are successful in throwing the aggressor off of you, immediately go into your ground defence fighting position (see Figures 2.89 and 2.90).

Front Pin – Aggressor Inside Victim's Legs

You are on your back, pinned down by the assailant who is now between your legs (Figure 2.91).

To execute this defence manoeuvre, lie on the centre of your back. Raise your left leg up and over the

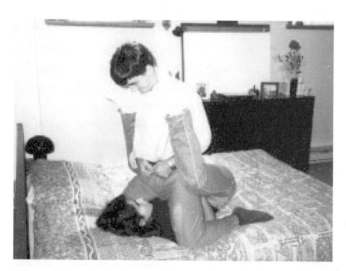

Figure 2.89. Front pin – seated

Figure 2.91. Front pin – inside victim's legs

Figure 2.93. Front pin – inside victim's legs

Figure 2.92. Front pin – inside victim's legs

assailant's head. There should be an opportunity to trap your instep under his chin or against his throat. Once your foot is in place, you will be able to push him away. Be sure that it is your back that is on the ground and that your buttocks are not. Lying on your back will give you more leverage as you swing your legs upward. Once you are successful in throwing the aggressor off of you, immediately go into your ground defence fighting position (see Figures 2.92 and 2.93).

Rear Pins

Being pinned face down on the ground is perhaps the worst case scenario. This situation should be avoided at all costs. When struggling in a confrontation on the ground, opponents sometimes have a tendency to roll over one another. Inexperienced individuals who are pinned down on their back can wrestle themselves into an even worse situation where they are pinned face down. This greatly reduces your options. When the aggressor is on top of you inside your legs and pinning you down, you will need to rely on your hips and lower body strength to throw him off. Slide your strongest leg, bent at the knee, upward as high as it will go. Remember to keep the inside of your knee on the ground (Figure 2.94).

Plant the sole of your foot onto the ground and twist your hips away from your leg into the aggressor. This should flip him off of you (Figure 2.95).

If he does not pin your arms down, the technique will be easy to implement. Use the hand opposite your strongest leg to help push the aggressor off by placing your elbow in his neck or facial area while twisting towards him (Figure 2.96). Once you are successful in throwing the aggressor off of you, immediately go into your ground defence fighting position (see Figure 2.77).

STANDING STRANGLE AND CHOKE RELEASES

Front Choke – Two Arms or One Arm on Victim's Neck

In this situation, the victim is being choked with two hands by the aggressor (Figure 2.97).

To execute this technique properly you will need

Figure 2.94. Rear pin

Figure 2.95. Rear pin

Figure 2.96. Rear pin

your raised right arm to break your assailant's hold on your neck (Figure 2.99).

As your right arm crosses over the aggressor's arms, breaking his hold, maintain a grip on his left wrist with your left hand. Remember that it is the movement of the raised right arm (inside biceps area), as you turn your hips, that causes the release of the opponent's grip. You should be able to trap both his arms between your upper arm (back part of arm or triceps) and your ribcage (Figure 2.100).

Hold on tightly to both arms while they are trapped with your left hand. Chamber your right elbow and deliver a reverse roundhouse elbow strike to the opponent's face or neck area. This is done by moving your right hand across so that it touches your left ear (Figure 2.101).

To strike, simply extend the elbow to its target. If you cannot reach the aggressor's face or neck with your elbow, unfold it keeping your arm slightly bent, to allow your forearm to strike the target. You should have an opportunity to strike at your target several times as his hands should remain trapped in your armpit (Figure 2.102).

The most common mistake that students make when learning this technique is that they bend their backs as they twist their hips. The back does not bend downward, it stays upright. If you have difficulty twisting your upper body, focus on a spot on the wall directly behind you at the start of this technique. When you begin to twist your upper body do not turn your head. Only pivot from the waist and remember not to bend your back downward. Keep

to have space behind you. This particular technique will not work if you are being choked against a wall. To escape a two-handed choke, you will once again need to deliver the techniques with surprise, precision, and speed. Grab the aggressor's left wrist with your left hand. Make certain that your arm is over both of his arms and not between them. As you grip his wrist, take a step back with your left foot in a semi-circle so that your left foot is directly behind your right front foot (Figure 2.98).

This is likely to pull the aggressor slightly off balance. Keep your knees slightly bent. Next, you will have to raise your right arm straight up as you turn (twist) your hips. Your entire upper body will twist (your right hip should twist in the direction towards the opponent) from your waist allowing

Figure 2.97. Front choke

Figure 2.98. Front choke

Figure 2.99. Front choke

Figure 2.100. Front choke

Figure 2.101. Front choke

Figure 2.102. Front choke

twisting until you see the spot on the wall. Do not get discouraged if you experience difficulty with this technique; it is one of the more difficult ones described here.

Front Choke – Against a Wall

Perhaps the most effective strategy to implement in this situation is the thumbing eye gouge and groin kick (Figures 2.103 and 2.104).

Another option would be to trap the offender's arms by bringing both of your arms upward and inside, breaking his hold on your neck (Figures 2.105 and 2.106).

Your arms would then wrap around his arms, trapping them in under your arms. Follow up with a head butt (Figure 2.107).

Rear Choke – Two Arm or One Arm on Victim's Neck

To escape this scenario you will have to go in the direction that the aggressor is pushing or pulling you. If he is attempting to push you forward, take a step forward with your right foot (Figure 2.108).

Raise your left arm straight up and twist your upper body (above your waist only) around towards the attacker. You should be moving in the direction of your rear leg as you pivot on the balls of your feet. You will only be able to twist one way (Figure 2.109).

You should not only break his grip but also have an opportunity to trap his arms by wrapping your left arm over and around both of his arms (Figure 2.110).

Figure 2.103. Choke against a wall

Figure 2.105. Choke against a wall

Figure 2.104. Choke against a wall

Figure 2.106. Choke against a wall

Resistance Alternatives   95

Figure 2.107. Choke against a wall

Figure 2.108. Rear choke

Keeping his arms trapped, you may have the opportunity to readjust and deliver several groin kicks to the aggressor (Figure 2.111).

If he has a great deal of momentum, such as if he would be running towards you, it may be virtually impossible to trap his arms, but you will still be able to break his hold.

Rear Choke – One Arm around Victim's Mouth or Neck

The aggressor approaches you from behind. He grabs you from around the neck cutting into your air supply at the throat with his arm. Turning your head sideways into the crook of his elbow may increase your oxygen supply and reduce the impact of the initial strangle (Figure 2.112).

Figure 2.109. Rear choke

Figure 2.110. Rear choke

Figure 2.112. Rear choke

Figure 2.111. Rear choke

Figure 2.113. Rear choke

Figure 2.114. Rear choke

Do not try to use your strength to wrestle out of the hold. Deliver a forearm groin strike, or implement a groin grab (Figures 2.113 and 2.114).

You may also choose to implement other strategies involving a variety of leg strikes. A swift heel stomp to the aggressor's instep or a quick back kick to his knee joint may deter him from his goal.

Head Lock Defence
In this situation the aggressor has taken hold of your neck while standing beside you. He bends forward putting pressure on your neck. As you bend forward into this position, immediately strike the groin region with either hand. You may also choose to reach back with the arm closest to the aggressor.

The arm should travel upward over the aggressor's head, just under his nose (Figures 2.115 and 2.116).

Use your small outside finger to put pressure on the bridge of his nose. Be sure to support the small finger with the remaining fingers by keeping the hand flexed open. Another option is to grab hold of his hair and pull it back as you continue to strike his groin with your other hand.

DEFENCE AGAINST STANDING HOLDS

Front Bear Hug – Arms Trapped
In this situation the aggressor is hugging you with his arms around your waist. Your arms are trapped inside his grip. You have several options in this situation. You may choose to strike the groin with your knee, or perhaps execute a groin grab. A head butt could also be an effective response.

Front Bear Hug – Arms Free
To escape from this hold simply open both of your hands and slap them against his ears (Figures 2.117 and 2.118).

Delivering a thumbing eye gouge would also be one of the more effective techniques to consider. Another option may be to resort to a palm strike. As you apply this palm strike to the chin, you should cause the opponent's head to move backward (Figure 2.119).

You may choose to implement a 'head twist.' As you apply a palm strike, grab his hair at the back of his head and apply a twisting and pulling motion. Pull him back in a downward motion in the same

Figure 2.115. Head lock

Figure 2.117. Front bear hug

Figure 2.116. Head lock

Figure 2.118. Front bear hug

Figure 2.119. Front bear hug

Figure 2.120. Front bear hug

direction as your palm strike. If this technique is done properly, the aggressor may lose his balance and fall to the floor (Figure 2.120).

Rear Bear Hug – Arms Trapped
This defence technique can also be used to counter the rear bear hug around your waist and arms (Figure 2.121).

First, to distract the aggressor, execute a quick heel stomp on his instep. Then you will need to lock both your hands tightly together. Next, you will need to squat down until your thighs are parallel to the ground, simultaneously straightening out your arms with an upward movement (Figure 2.122).

This technique should allow you the opportunity to slip out of his hold. Be careful to keep your back straight. Do not fall to your knees, stay on your feet keeping you thighs parallel with the ground. Execute a forearm groin strike as a follow-up technique.

Hands Trapped in Standing Neck Lock – Take-Down Option
In this scenario, the aggressor stands behind you and traps your hands in an upward position between your neck and shoulders, while forcing your neck forward (Figure 2.123).

To escape from this technique, place your right leg, using an outside movement, behind the calf of his left leg. If done properly, your shin should be in contact with his calf. You will have to slightly pivot your right hip and leg behind the aggressor's left leg for this manoeuvre to work properly (Figure 2.124).

Figure 2.121. Rear bear hug

Figure 2.122. Rear bear hug

Figure 2.123. Standing neck lock

Lean back towards that leg, sending his body weight over his trapped leg. He will lose his balance and likely release his hold or fall to the ground (Figure 2.125).

Hands Trapped in Standing Neck Lock – Slip-Out Option

Another option in this situation, if the take-down option does not work for you, is the slip-out option. You will need to straighten out your arms as you raise them straight upward. Simultaneously, bend at the knees while keeping your back straight and

Figure 2.124. Standing neck lock

Figure 2.125. Standing neck lock

slip out of the hold. Your thighs should be parallel to the ground. Follow up with a forearm strike to the groin (Figures 2.126 and 2.127).

DIRTY TRICKS AND OTHER DEFENSIVE STRATEGIES

If you are ever the subject of a violent attack and choose to use physical resistance, you need to know that you can do whatever it takes to help you defend yourself and survive the experience. Until now the focus has been on effective conventional techniques that can be applied rather easily if practised on a regular basis. This section focuses on the strategies that are sometimes overlooked. The following should be considered as effective alternatives for various situations

Biting
There are several situations when biting may be an effective option. This is primarily a close range defence technique. Therefore, if you are out of bitting

Figure 2.126. Standing neck lock

Figure 2.127. Standing neck lock

range, it would be better to stay out of that range and execute another technique such as a kick or hand strike. It would not be wise to move in closer to the opponent than you already are. A common situation in which a biting technique may be used is when the aggressor is pulling you in close for a kiss. Your target may include his nose, cheek, chin, lip, tongue, or ear. This will all depend upon what is available at that particular moment. Although this technique can cause a great deal of pain and be extremely effective in deterring the aggressor, biting your assailant may subject you to contracting the HIV virus as well as other diseases including hepatitis. To execute this technique simply bite through the target with the goal of severing it from his body (Figure 2.128).

Ear Twist
This is an effective, yet simple, self-defence technique which requires you to grab each of your

Figure 2.128. Biting

Figure 2.129. Ear twist

aggressor's ears with each of your hands. Simply turn and twist his head sideways in a downward motion bringing him to the ground (Figure s 2.129 and 2.130).

Scratching

Although pinching the aggressor is not highly recommended, scratching him is beneficial especially if you decide to prosecute him. Scratching him will trap DNA evidence under your fingernails that will help identify him in court.

Head Butting – Front

This is a violent manoeuvre usually used by street brawlers. It involves a simple, quick movement whereby you strike the facial area of the aggressor

Figure 2.130. Ear twist

Figure 2.131. Head butting

with the top part of your forehead. Usually you would be aiming for his nose (Figure 2.131).

As with biting, this is a close range option to be used particularly when someone is pulling you close to him. The technique must be done quickly, catching the opponent by surprise. You must pull the opponent in towards you quickly as you butt your head.

Head Butting – Backward

It is possible to use the head butt to strike a rear target. Again, it is to be used at very close range. If your aggressor grabs you from the rear and pulls you in close, it may be a good option. Your target once again is the facial area. You may choose to aim directly at the nose. You would need to send the back of your head crashing into his nose in a very quick movement. Be careful not to hesitate when delivering the strike. Any hesitation may tip off the opponent, and you may lose the element of surprise.

Finger Twists

Finger twists are not the most elegant selection in the repertoire of self-defence techniques, but they still provide an effective way to deal with an aggressive person. As you probably realize, fingers are not meant to be bent backward. With the rare exception of individuals who are double-jointed, bending a finger backward against the joint will cause pain. You may wish to resort to gripping a finger and bending backward to entice an aggressor to release his hold. This is not a lethal technique. The pain that you cause the opponent may antagonize him to display further violence. Perhaps this option works best with intoxicated co-workers at a company Christmas party, or an aggressive date in a public place. It may be useful to focus on the aggressor's baby finger. Simply grip it firmly with your hand and twist it back. The baby finger is the aggressor's weakest finger and it will be hard for him to resist the twist.

Wrist Twists

This technique is more of a control manoeuvre. As the opponent comes near you or grabs your left shoulder with his right hand, grab that hand with both of your hands twisting it using a counter-clockwise motion as far as it will go (Figures 2.132 to 2.134).

Simultaneously step back with your left leg and

twist your hips towards your left side as well. You should be moving in a circular motion while you maintain the wrist lock on the aggressor. You should be able to pull him off balance, sending him to the floor, as you continue to turn (Figures 2.136 and 2.137).

While executing this technique, it is important to keep the opponent's hand close to your body. Remember that you need to use your hips to make this technique work. As you twist his hand, keeping it close to your body, you will need to twist your hips. This movement should pull him off balance. This is a very difficult technique to learn from a book. It should require more time to understand and perfect than most of the other techniques.

Most sexual assaults occur near a home or a car. In this environment, there are natural obstacles and other barriers that may be able to help the victim. You should be aware of these elements. Lighting conditions are one issue that may be a factor in an attack situation. Can you see your offender? Consider a young woman's experience of how she was assaulted on her college campus: 'I had gone out for the evening to study for a final exam with some classmates. I arrived home in the late evening hours. I went to sleep that evening and was awoken by an intruder who had gained entry to my apartment through an open window. I really never saw him. He put duct tape over my eyes. I attempted to fight him off. During the struggle, I was knocked unconscious' (anonymous victim, paraphrased).

Once you have mastered some of the basic tech-

Figure 2.132. Wrist twist

Figure 2.133. Wrist twist

Figure 2.134. Wrist twist

Figure 2.136. Wrist twist

Figure 2.135. Wrist twist

Figure 2.137. Wrist twist

pin-and-strangle defences. When fighting an opponent who you cannot see, never let him out of your grasp. This is the only way to be certain of where he is. Also, try to learn the layout of your apartment or house so that you can escape in the dark, if necessary.

Makeshift weapons in your home could serve as useful objects. There may be many items that can be used to successfully deter the aggressor in your home. Lamps, pots, a telephone, even a plastic pen can be used as weapons. Objects may also be thrown at exterior windows, as the sounds of the breaking glass may help summon the assistance of caring neighbours and authorities. Such an action may also catch the aggressor off guard, and the sounds of breaking glass may scare him away. Kitchen tables and other large pieces of furniture can be used as obstacles to separate you from the aggressor.

Terrain is another element to consider and prepare for. Your self-defence efforts may be affected by the environment of where the attack might occur. For instance, it might be easier to break out of a floor pin in your front yard on wet ground then on a carpeted floor in your bedroom, or in your bed where your body weight will sink into the mattress. Pavement might be extremely difficult to execute ground techniques on since the surface is hard and coarse. Other areas that deserve special consideration include the showers and bathrooms since these surfaces provide hard and often slippery surfaces. Some experts advise that if a confrontation is imminent in this area, a woman should go immediately into a ground defence position. Perhaps it would be best to first attempt to persuade the aggressor out of this area. If a situation arises where you are showering and do have an opportunity to escape, do not stop to dress. You must exit the dangerous area as quickly as possible.

If attacked in your car, there are a couple of effective options you have. If you are in your car and an aggressor approaches you in an attempt to grab you through the window, roll the window up on his hands. This is an especially effective strategy if your car is equipped with power windows. If the aggressor approaches your door and it seems that a confrontation is unavoidable, open your car door just slightly and place your left foot against the door. Your knee should be bent in close to your body, similar to a chambered leg before a kick (see leg strike section). As he comes in range kick out violently on the door sending it directly into his knees. Be ready to implement a follow-up strike (Figures 2.138 to 2.140).

Closing the car door on the aggressor's hand, foot, fingers, or arm may also prove to be a resourceful strategy. If you are abducted in a car, you may wish to draw attention to your situation by crashing into another car in a busy area at a low speed; a good choice might be a police car.

Weapons

It would not be appropriate to discuss weapon defences in great detail. When a weapon is present, it changes many aspects of the altercation. With an armed attacker, the likelihood of danger automati-

Figure 2.138. In your car

Figure 2.140. In your car

Figure 2.139. In your car

cally increases. You may choose to physically resist your aggressor. This should be considered if you believe that the aggressor is actually committed in using the weapon, rather than using it as a threat. However, it should not be your first option. Escaping from this situation should be your main goal. Accompanying the aggressor to a second location is likely to put you at greater risk since it will be a more isolated environment. Never leave the primary crime scene under any circumstances. If you choose to resist, you will need to control the weapon before neutralizing the assailant. It should be emphasized that physical resistance should not be used to protect material possessions – only to protect your life. Submitting to the attack may be your safest alternative. This is a personal decision that you will have to make. Some factors that may aid in your decision include the same factors mentioned earlier (the location of the crime, the personality of the offender, the personality of the victim). Also, you may consider if a weapon has actually been displayed to you, or is it being concealed. These types of situations can be very unpredictable.

Using a weapon for personal protection is generally not recommended since there are many cases in which the aggressor ends up using the victim's weapon against her. If you choose to carry a weapon, check first with your local law enforcement agency to determine what is legal in your area. You will need to consider if you feel comfortable using a weapon against another person before an incident occurs. Mace and pepper sprays are perhaps the best options, but certain types of sprays may be illegal in your area. Proper care of the product is necessary. Outdated or poorly maintained devices could create a false sense of security for the user. Periodically (i.e., on a monthly basis) shake the mace canister and check the expiration date It is recommended that you learn how to use the weapon properly. For example, spraying pepper spray at your aggressor on a windy day may likely incapacitate you rather than him. If you plan on carrying mace on you, buy an extra canister to practise with. If you plan to keep this weapon in your purse, you will have to be extra careful that children in your household do not have access to it. Generally carrying any type of weapon or personal safety device is not very practical. It is likely that you will not have it with you at all times. It may be effective in deterring a stranger aggressor on the street. However, it has been mentioned that the majority of aggressive acts are caused by people we know and trust. You are not likely to have your personal safety devices ready in such intimate situations. Furthermore, if the device does not work for you, you will have no other option. Do not become dependent on anything or anybody other than yourself.

DEFENDING YOURSELF AGAINST MULTIPLE ASSAILANTS

When dealing with multiple attackers, try not to be cornered into a situation where you have no escape. If they have already engaged you in interaction, do not deviate from the direction that you were headed in. Stand firm and be assertive. If an assault begins to take place, you may choose to focus your resistance on the leader. Place yourself with your back against a wall so that you avoid a surprise attack from the rear. Focus all your resistance efforts on the leader. Do not take your eyes off the leader; it is essential that you stay focused on him. Avoid meaningless conversation and request that they leave you alone. Try not to be drawn by slight touch as this is a strategy to test your reactions. If you begin to lose control and this situation turns into a 'beating' attack, you will most likely be on the ground. Lie on your side with your back to a wall. Tuck your head in towards your chest covering it with your arms. Assume a fetal position bending your knees in close to your mid-section. This will protect your head, back, and major internal organs.

AFTER AN ATTACK

Immediately after an attack:

- Go to a safe place.
- Call for help, consider reporting the crime to the police.

You may choose to report the incident to the police. If you wish, or are undecided, do not change anything about your body or the crime scene. Do not wash, shower, bathe, douche, comb your hair, smoke, or eat or drink anything. Doing any of these things could destroy valuable evidence needed to convict the aggressor. Although it may be important to collect this type of physical evidence to prove sexual relations, it will not be helpful in addressing whether or not the victim consented. If you choose to file a police report, it will be helpful to remember what the perpetrator looks like. Figure 2.141 may be useful in helping you keep track of his description.

- Seek medical care depending on the nature of the assault and injuries sustained.

Whether you report the aggressor or not, you should seek medical care after an attack. Consider bringing a friend along for support. Consider calling a rape crisis centre for information and support.

Common reactions to sexual assault can include emotional trauma. The person may experience feelings of being dirty. She may feel anger, shock, hu-

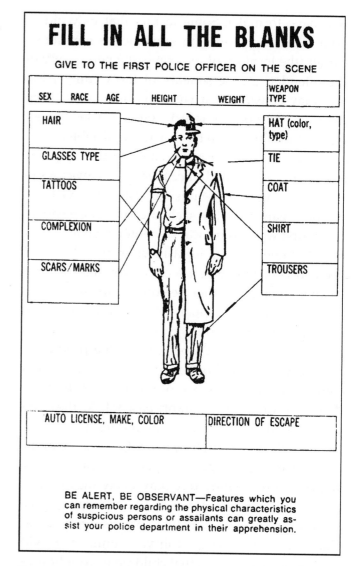

Figure 2.141. Suspect description. Courtesy of the Chicago Police Department

miliation, denial, or disbelief. Many rape survivors blame themselves, as they wonder what they had done to provoke the violence. Victims may suffer from loss of self-esteem. This may result in depression, mood swings, substance abuse, or suicide. They may become withdrawn and severely limit their social contact with others. Flashbacks of the rape can also be experienced.

A rape survivor may have difficulty interacting with males, especially on an interpersonal level. She may no longer feel secure in her environment (i.e., school, work, and home). Some victims develop eating disorders such as nausea, appetite loss, or overeating. Sleep disorders such as insomnia and intense frequent nightmares may also be experienced. It is strongly recommended that rape victims consider counselling after an attack.

Helping a Rape Survivor
Listen and believe her story. Do not judge her. Offer her support and comfort. Let the victim know that you care and that you want to help. Be patient and supportive. Let the person decide what type of help she wants from you. The victim must make her own decisions. You can listen and offer suggestions and encouragement. It is important to stress that the victim is not to blame, and that it is not at all her fault.

FINDING A GOOD SCHOOL IN YOUR AREA

This book should provide you with a comprehensive basic overview of personal safety and self-defence education. It should not be used as a substitute for hands-on instruction. If you are interested learning self-defence on a deeper level, you will need to find the proper type of school. The Montreal-based White Tiger Street Defence offers specialized workshops in women's self-defence instruction throughout most areas of Quebec, Ontario, New York, and New England for schools, colleges, corporate groups, and police agencies. However, if you are considering enrolling in a course type of program individually, there are a few points worth considering. Self-defence, although it is based on the principles of martial arts, is something very different. Genuine women's self-defence programs should be specially developed to meet the specific needs of women. Martial arts schools are not regulated or licensed in most parts of North America. Schools may belong to professional organizations where they pay an annual membership fee. This does not necessarily mean much. In reality, anyone can open a school or start a new style of martial arts academy even with little or no experience at all, just as easily as opening up a small business. You should be aware that the type of school that you are searching for will be extremely rare and probably slightly more expensive than your neighbourhood karate school. It is possible that you will not find the school you need in your town or community.

Be wary of karate schools who *also* claim to teach self-defence. Most martial arts schools that teach traditional disciplines such as tae kwon do or karate do not teach the type of techniques that you will find useful during an assault. Many instructors 'sell' themselves as experts as they refer to the number of trophies that they have won in regional or national competitions for fighting or for kata (non-contact form of display). You will need to stay away from schools that practise fancy high spinning kicks or offer little or no contact fighting. Even well-intentioned instructors will usually be ineffective because the type of self-defence that you are searching for requires a great deal of specialization. You will need to find a school that specializes in practical and non-traditional fighting techniques. This school typically would not participate with other schools in competitive sport events. Many instructors have very big egos just as every student in the martial arts believes that their style of martial art is the best. This will definitely not help you as you search for an appropriate school. You should not be obligated to join initially. Ask the instructor for a couple of free trial classes. Once you find the right school, you should not have to sign a contract committing to a term longer than three months. Many schools offer monthly membership options. Most martial arts schools operate on a belt rank system. It may take up to five years to attain senior belt status. Various colours are used to represent the various levels of expertise. Most of these systems presuppose that the student has an infinite amount of time to acquire and perfect their skill. Be extremely cautious about schools that advertise being a black belt in a certain amount of time. Equally important is that once you find what appears to be an appropriate school, you should ask about the instructors' credentials and experience.

Specialized Schools

Typically, the self-defence instructors and organizations that are likely to meet your needs are limited. Specialized schools should practise all of the general elements presented in this book. Role plays involving a male aggressor in which female participants have an opportunity to practise keeping a safe distance while executing their verbal skills is an essential element of any quality oriented self-defence course for women. There should be the opportunity for full contact scenarios where female participants can practise fighting off a male aggressor. Good quality organizations base their content on academic research whenever possible, and examine other alternatives besides physical resistance.

Program Length

Most specialized self-defence programs are highly structured. The entire program may range from three to twenty-four hours or more, with the general average being between six to ten hours. Students in a shorter program are not likely to be mentally or physically prepared for a full contact drill at the end of the program. However, shorter programs of about four hours serve as a good introduction and are also an excellent tool to sensitize high school and college students to the self-defence issue. Seminar training should be a minimum of about three hours. Another good option would be breaking apart the seminar by offering half on one day and half on the next. Although the padded assailant can be used to enhance this basic seminar, it is only after six to seven hours of instruction that it would be appropriate to introduce the students into full contact scenarios.

Equally dangerous are the intensive programs that offer a ten- to twelve-hour course over a period of two days. Imagine what the memory retention of the course information would be under these circumstances. Instruction should not exceed four hours per day. I have seen many of these programs set up in high schools on professional days as an extra school-based activity. Programs set up in this fashion can be dangerous since the participants do not have the opportunity to practise the movements on their own, with the chance to review their mistakes in the next class. This may create a false sense of security for the participants. While it is always commendable when teachers and parents realize the proactive need for assault prevention training, it is virtually useless, if it is offered in this way. Ideally this eight to twelve-hour program should be spread out, offered once or twice weekly for periods of four hours or less. The longer the total time frame is between the sessions, the more beneficial the program will be. Therefore, twelve to fifteen hours offered in three days is not as meaningful as twelve to fifteen hours offered over six weeks. Quality oriented courses should not provide key chain batons in plastic, metal, or wood to their participants, as this instills confidence in an object rather than their own natural ability to defend themselves. It is unlikely that a course participant will have keys in her hand in a potentially dangerous situation.

MALE OR FEMALE INSTRUCTORS

The traditional male karate instructor has been built into an intimidating macho stereotype in our society. Often female students will not relate as well, or ask questions that need to be asked in a traditional martial arts type environment. I would like to think that it is the sensitivity, performance, and knowledge of an instructor rather than his sex that makes him a good women's self-defence instructor. Male instructors who are properly trained and have the right attitude are very useful in simulating aggressive situations for participants. The padded male assailant enhances the program because women can actually strike vulnerable body targets with full force. This adds a sense of realism to the program.

Female instructors should also be an essential part of the course. It is very empowering to the participants to see women as role models leading the class, especially in high school level courses. A preferable approach is to have a male and female instructor involved in every class of the course so that students can benefit from both.

REALISTIC TEACHING METHODOLOGY

Learning self-defence skills comes from constant repetition. Although the techniques at first will seem mechanical, with the proper amount of practise they will become natural movements. First, programs should centre equally on teaching how to resist an aggressor. This involves all of the various types of strategies mentioned in this book. Second, and equally important, is the element of teaching participants the context in which these crimes occur. A realistic approach means a hands-on interactive approach where the participants are comfortable enough to ask sensitive questions without hesitation. With physical resistance, this involves realistic training drills, role plays, and full contact scenarios with a padded male aggressor. Students should be offered regular feedback on their performance. A teacher–student ratio should not exceed one to fifteen.

A major downfall with traditional self-defence programs is that they fail to meet the specific self-protection needs of most women. It has been mentioned that real self-defence is comprised of many other elements in addition to physical resistance. The best and most accurate advice that can be offered is based on current academic studies such as the ones cited throughout this book. In setting up prevention programs, it is best to have a multidimensional approach to the issue. No one agency, teacher or police department should be led to believe that they have a monopoly on crime prevention in their community. Pride should be taken in the establishment of solid, well-working initiatives between various prevention experts. Ideally, these types of partnerships should be sponsored by local businesses.

References

Bart, P., and P. O'Brien. (1985). *Stopping Rape: Successful Survival Strategies*. New York: Pergamon.

Bateman P. (1990). *Teen Sex: Drawing the Line*. Seattle: Alternatives to Fear.

Browder, S. (1985, Jan.). *'Social Rape: When Seduction Turns to Horror.'* *Cosmopolitan*, 150–3.

Brozan, N. (1986, Feb. 17). 'Gang Rape: A Rising Campus Concern.' *New York Times*, 17.

Citrano, H. (1994). Unpublished information provided based on reported crimes on campus, University of California at Los Angeles, UCLA Campus Police.

Cooper City Police. (1997). 'Rohypnol: The Date Rape Drug.' *Cooper City Police Department Crime Report*. Cooper City, Forida.

Davidson, A. (1994). 'Alcohol, Drugs, and Family violence.' *Violence Update, 4(5)*, 5–6.

Dutton, D.G. (1995). *The Batterer: A Psychological Profile*. New York: Basic Books.

Harpold, J.A. (1996) 'Sexual Assault Awareness.' Unpublished presentation for United Against Crime Telecast, Fort Worth, Texas.

Hazelwood, R.R. (1983) 'The Behavior Oriented Interview of Rape Victims: The Key to Profiling.' *FBI Law Enforcement Bulletin*. Reprinted in The National Center for the Analysis of Violent Crime (NCAVC). *Deviant Sexuality*. Quantico, Va: Author (1991), 231–8.

– and J.A. Harpold (1986) 'Rape: The Dangers of Providing Confrontational Advice.' *FBI Law Enforcement Bulletin*. Reprinted in The National Center for the Analysis of Violent Crime (NCAVC). *Deviant Sexuality*. Quantico, Va: Author (1991), 225–9.

Houseman, R. (1993) *Unleash the Lioness: A Women's Guide to Fighting Off Violent Attack*. London: Houlder and Stoughton.

Jacobson, N. (1993, Oct.). 'Domestic Violence: What Are the Marriages Like?' American Association for Marriage and Family Therapy. Anaheim, California.

Kleck, G., and S. Sayles. (1990). 'Rape and Resistance.' *Social Problems, 37(2)*, 149–62.

Koss, M.P., T.E. Dinero, C.A. Seibel, and S.L. Cox. (1988). 'Stranger and Acquaintance Rape: Are There Differences in the Victim's Experience?' *Psychology of Women Quarterly, 12*, 1–24.

Lenskyj, H. (1992). *An Analysis of Violence against Women: A Manual for Educators and Administrators*. Toronto: Institute for the Studies in Education.

Marvin, M.J. (ed.). (1995). *Preventing Violence against Women: Not Just a Women's Issue*. Washington: National Crime Prevention Council.

McIntyre, J.J. (1980). 'Victim Response to Rape Alternative Outcomes.' Final report of grant MH 29045, *National Institute of Mental Health*.

McNamara, J.D. (1984). *Safe and Sane: The Sensible Way to Protect Yourself, Your Loved Ones, Your Property and Possessions*. New York: Perigee.

Muehlenhard, C.L. and M.A. Linton. (1987). 'Date Rape and Sexual Aggression in Dating Situations: Incidence and Risk Factors.' *Journal of Counseling Psychology, 34(2)*, 186–96.

Rogers, K. (1994, Fall). 'Wife Assault in Canada,' *Canadian Social Trends*. Ottawa: Statistics Canada. 3–14.

Tempe Police Department. (1990). *Sexual Assault Survival Course Handbook*. Tempe, Arizona: author.

Ullman, S.E. and R.A. Knight. (1995). 'Women's Resistance Strategies to Different Rapist Types.' *American Journal of Public Health, 22(3)*, 263–83.

– (1992). 'Fighting Back: Women's Resistance to Rape.' *Journal of Interpersonal Violence, 7*, 31–43.

Warshaw, R. (1988). *I Never Called It Rape*. New York: Harper and Row.

Zoucha-Jensen, M. and A. Coyne. (1993). 'The Effects of Resistance Strategies on Rape.' *American Journal of Public Health, 83(11)*, 1633–4.

Index

About the Author

Paul Henry Danylewich has been involved in martial arts and self-defence for over ten years. He founded White Tiger Street Defense, a personal safety school for women and children in April of 1993 when his martial arts hobby began to bridge with his academic interests in the field of sexual aggression and deviance. Paul remains the director of White Tiger Street Defense. The organization provides seminars and courses throughout parts of Canada and the United States on assault prevention, and offers special consulting services to stalking victims. He holds a university degree in sociology and education, and a graduate degree in adult education from Concordia University in Montreal. With a continual commitment to developing assault prevention programs upon an academic framework, efforts are made so that participants recognize and understand the context in which these crimes occur. Paul often attends and gives presentations on personal safety and 'safe schools' strategies to police officers, teachers, parents, and students. He has recently been accredited as a Crime Prevention Specialist by the New York State Crime Prevention Coalition (Albany, NY). Paul is also a freelance writer and has contributed to various police journals and women's magazines.

Paul Henry Danylewich and White Tiger Street Defense offer personal safety seminars and workshops for groups, companies, schools, colleges, and police agencies. The group also offers personal consultations concerning stalking deterrence strategies and threat management services. All services are available in most parts of Quebec, Ontario, New York, and New England. For more information, contact Paul Henry Danylewich by writing or calling White Tiger Street Defense at the following address:

Paul Henry Danylewich, Director
White Tiger Street Defense
4944 Decarie Boulevard, Suite 212
Montreal, Quebec, Canada, H3X 3T4
tel: (514) 685-8888
tel: 1-877-685-8880 (toll free in Canada)
fearlesstiger@hotmail.com
www.geocities/paulhenrydanylewich